REBOUNDING

FROM

HOMELESSNESS

How to Forgive Through the Process

SHEILA POPE, Ph.D.

New Beginnings Media & Publishing

An imprint of Pope's Resource Center, LLC

New Beginnings Media & Publishing, Pearland, 77581

An imprint of Pope's Resource Center, LLC © 2021 by Sheila Pope

This title is also available as a Pope's Resource Center, LLC hardcoverbook.

This title is also available as a Pope's Resource Center, LLC paperbackbook.

Requests for information should be addressed to:

Pope's Resource Center, LLC, P.O. Box 1744 Pearland, TX 77588 www.popesresourcecenterllc.com

ISBN 978-0-578-92541-7 (HC)

Scripture quotations are taken from the Holy Bible, King James Version.

A catalog record for this book is available from the Library of Congress. Printed in the United States of America

To Christopher, Matthew, Taylor, and London God has given me four reasons to get up and trust him to make me a better mother, founder, and christian.

Contents

Chapter 1

The Tremont Hotel

To finish writing my story, I decided to return to The Tremont House Hotel in Galveston, TX, on April 11th, 2021. On April 10th, 2021, I traveled to Galveston to secure a room for the entire weekend; however, things did not turn out as I had hoped. It was almost impossible to get a room at the hotel because Galveston was packed with people (see Figure 1). The rates for rooms were double their usual cost, and I could not understand why it was so challenging to secure a space anywhere. It seemed to have slipped my mind that Governor Greg Abbott, on March 2nd, 2021, reopened Texas 100 percent and lifted mask requirements. Also, people were still receiving their second round of stimulus checks, so they were able to enjoy a beautiful weekend without masks, without six feet distance rules, and with a bit of extra money to spend time relaxing with their family and friends.

FIGURE 1. Dr. Pope at the Tremont Hotel on April 11, 2021. Photo by Author

When I decided to pack up and drive to Galveston without a plan,

I kept replaying my memories of my time at The Tremont House. My desire to finish organizing my book drove my determination to go there again.

When I write, I have zones or moments when I know it's time to focus on finishing up a project. I decided on April 11th, I was going to travel to the one place that made me feel like I could write a book. On May 17th, 2017, I attended Houston Community College's Faculty Retreat held at the Tremont. At that time, I was an adjunct English Professor for the college. I was so excited because the college paid for my room, and I was away from my children. I stayed in room 210. As I walked into the room, I saw myself writing a book.

In May 2017, I was alive and very aware of the physical and mental changes I was experiencing at 48. I had left my job as a teacher in an urban school district. I was filled with hope in 2017 at The Tremont House Hotel (see Figure 2). I was open to doing something new with my life. I knew I would write a book at the hotel, but I did not have a story to tell in 2017. By April 11th, 2021, my life changed four years later, and I had enough experience writing multiple books.

Earl Simmons, known as the rapper DMX and one of my favorite rappers, died on April 9th, 2021, after a long battle with drugs and alcohol. He had a brief fight with COVID-19, but a drug overdose was the official cause of his death (Vulture, 2021). DMX had several heart attacks and never recovered. I watched a clip from DMX and Snoop Dogg's Verzuz on July 22nd, 2020. After performing the song "Slippin" (Simons, 1998), DMX told Snoop Dogg, "You have to write your pain! Write your pain!" (Simmons, Earl, Verzuz, 2020)! He said he wanted to share his pain with other young men to avoid his pitfalls and pain (Simmons, Earl Verzuz 2020)! I felt like God had allowed me to hear DMX's words again. After his death, I listened to his songs with a different intention, and his words resonated with me.

I had to use a different method to write this book because the pain I experienced was excruciating. I cried when I listened to the audios I recorded. I cried when I looked at different photos. I cried when I saw

Facebook memories from two years ago. I knew how far God had helped me progress, but I still remembered the pain behind my smiles. I cried while I typed my thoughts and words in different chapters of this book. I had to take breaks while I wrote this book. My intervals were sometimes months because it hurt to sit back down and face the fact, I lost my identity of being an "excellent" teacher in 2016 and a proud single black female homeowner in 2019. My experience writing this book was unlike writing educational material. There was a time when I could not sit for hours and edit and re-write papers. My heart had never been in my academic writing.

Chapter 2

Transformation

From February 2014 until December 2017, I worked with at-risk African American and Latino students at a high school. By February, I was my students' second teacher. The principal loved the school, and he had plans to turn it around. He became ill and died at the beginningof my second year at the school.

The seniors I taught were book and street-smart, but some were difficult to deal with because of their life experiences and jaded attitudes. I had to learn how to work with them, and they had to learn how to deal with my demands, personality, and expectations. I had to accept my students' attitudes, poor attendance, and low expectations. Our classes were interrupted due to threats from rival gangs, and students would fight anywhere for any reason.

When I started work at high school, my students challenged me at every juncture. I taught English, Pre-Advanced Placement English, Advanced Placement English, and English IV during my second year. I always believed I had the best and brightest students in the building. When I told other educators where I worked, they would smile and give me a look. Some would question my logic, but I knew I was supposed to teach there. I left teaching at Texas Southern University to be more effective and make more money. I understood my students' grades did not always indicate what I knew about their potential. I was determined to succeed because I knew I was an excellent teacher. Over time, my students began to believe they were the best students in the building. They performed well on their local and district benchmark assessment and other assessments like students who knew they were the best and brightest students. The change I did not expect was I grew to love my students like they were my own. I spent countless hours at games, events, and time with my students. More importantly, I grew to love their community too. I invested my time, money, and resources into my students and the community. I believed in the power of showing kindness, respect, love, consistency, and challenging my students. I saw myself in the female students.

I understood my female students at their core. I understood why they fought to the death. When I lived in a low-income apartment complex and was pushed too far, I would respond verbally or physically. I was always bold and fearless. I was book smart and likable, but deadly if you took my money or hit me. The girls in my classes were smart, always on defense mode. They had to be to survive in their community.

For three years, I had worked successfully with my students. I was confident in my teaching skills. I was the department chair, and my classes were used for "Show and Tell." In other words, when visitors came, they would walk them through my classes. I had almost 20 years of experience; I had been a counselor and an administrator for seven years. I knew school policy. More importantly, I knew when district policies were not being followed.

Moreover, I loved working with students with behavior challenges, and I was in the right place to flourish. It was stressful working in the school, but I understood why I was there until there was a change in the administration. I did not expect any real impact on my position. Before I knew it, I was in an unspoken battle with two administrators. I never knew what caused the problem, but I can tell you when I lost the war. The day I received a low evaluation on my walk-

9

through, I knew it was time to leave the building. The low score rocked me to my core. It touched on how I sawmyself. When I started working at the school, students called me B**ch

Almost every day, but the verbal attacks did not affect how I saw myself when I decided not to leave. I considered resigning due to my students' constant verbal attacks, but I knew who I was internally. My belief that I could win my students over allowed me to withstand and overcome those verbal blows. However, the unjustified low evaluation was earth-shattering for me. I could not let them go, nor could I turn my attitude around. I couldnot shut down the anger and disappointment.

Real Issues

It took me some time to understand my real issue with the evaluation. I realized my identity as an "excellent" teacher was linked tomy evaluation. I am an overachiever. I work to earn 100%, not 90%, on tests. I am the girl who decided to obtain five degrees, including a doctorate. I am a workaholic. I have always placed a high expectation on my performance in anything I attempt. I do not understand accepting below-average for any reason. I wondered why no other administrator questioned my evaluation. Why did the other administrators fail to advocate for me? I have not always been protected as a child and as an adult. I had put an excessive amount of time and resources into building relationships with the students and the community; however, the administration closed their eyes to the positive things that were happening in the English department. Evaluations were supposed to represent the bigger picture, and my evaluation was used as a weapon to harm and remind me of the new hierarchy. Although I wrote about hegemony in my dissertation, I was experiencing it for the first time in the workplace. I was not prepared, but I learned to recognize its subtle and forceful tactics through my experience while working at the high school.

I received teacher and administration evaluations with high marks in my teaching career, which has lasted for 20 years. I believed I was one of the best and brightest teachers. When I was hit with a two on my first walk-through evaluation by the new administrator, I wondered if the

10

administrator was aware of where we worked and who we were teaching. I thought she saw me as a weak teacher. From the first time the administrator gave me a two, I continued to believe that the administrator would recognize my value to the team and acknowledge my teaching skills over time. Then, when I received another low evaluation over and over until my final evaluation for the year was a two, I realized my evaluations were bricks used to hurt and destroy me professionally. I could not understand the logic of giving a two with no objective justification. Evaluations were tools designed to help teachers and administrators grow, reflect on their pedagogy. Evaluations protect teachers from hegemony.

Although I knew the purpose of an evaluation and understood the administrator's meaning in destroying me on paper, I became a victim of my anger. I harbored unforgiveness, and I lost trust in the administration team. I became enthralled in a battle against my own best interest. I wish I could say the evaluations were the only issues I faced. I faced other battles, but I believe the evaluations were the bricks that did the most damage to my identity.

My intelligence had always been one of my best assets, and this time, it became my body's enemy. Although I understood the administrator's plan to ensure I stayed in my place, I focused on the wrong issues. Fear crept into my mind, and I entertained it. I feared I would be stuck at that school because no one else would hire me because of my evaluation. Then, shame took a seat next to fear. They had a good time attacking my insecurities. I was ashamed of my evaluation scores. I knew that they did not reflect my teaching skills or effort, but I questioned myself and my identity. I also raged against the system that an administrator had the power to give me unwarranted low scores, and no one questioned their validity. The whole system was too crazy for me to accept.

Unfortunately, when I accepted and swallowed my thoughts, which were all lies, I dismissed all the good evolutions I earned before the new administrator arrived. I failed to think about all the teachers who had

11

come to the school and quit after two or three months because they could not endure the challenge I took and overcame. I hardly ever missed a day of work, and I would stay after school late most nights working. It got to a point my students would ask me to take a day off. I failed to focus on how my students grew and performed on benchmarks. Instead, I focused on the fact that I never received a two on any part of my evaluations in my entire teaching career. Ye, Kanye West, said hubris and anger are always riding close together while sharing his downfall on Drink Champs part 1 (West, Kanye, <u>Drink Champs, 2021</u>). I knew I was not the only teacher dealing with unfair evaluation, but I focused on my embarrassment, mistreatment, and disrespect. This type of thinking caused me to withdraw and overthink how to protect myself and win.

When May 2016 finally came, I was ready to fight and prove I was an excellent teacher. I was so hurt and angry that I was not easy to talk with anymore. My mother, a registered nurse, was the first to notice. Then, a good friend of mine, a Licensed Professional Counselor in Texas, commented on my intensity levels. I thought I could come back in August 2016 with a fresh attitude, but I failed to focus on my internal pain. I entertained my hurts, and I did not rest during the break. I kept looking at my evaluations and figuring out why God allowed them to happen. God was quiet during this time. All I heard was my pain and my ego. I could have resigned in May 2016, but I was determined not to allow the administration to run me off from my place of blessing. Intellects tend to believe they can think or solve every problem. When a premise is built on a mistaken belief, especially one based on an unsound argument, no amount of logic will lead to a solution because the idea was invalid from the start (Oxford Languages and Google, 2021). Walking away was the best solution, and it was an obvious solution. Unfortunately, my need to win, stay at the school to prove the administrators wrong and continue teaching my students almost destroyed me.

When we returned in August of 2016, we had our faculty meeting. The scores were back from STAAR testing. The principal announced my students had the highest growth on any testing area in the building on STAAR. The data showed what I already knew about my students: they were the best and the brightest. God redeemed my reputation with new data. My students' scores were 12 points higher than the previous year's test scores. Those evaluations were all lies. Yet my identity was still shattered. Based on my students' data, I was an excellent teacher. I should have celebrated harder than I did. I bought so much food and sodas for my students. They did the work to earn all the praise I gave them. My heart would not allow me to celebrate my win. I focused on the fact that I could not get any of the STAAR bonus money because of my evaluations. I gave my unforgiveness and anger another reason to keep thriving.

After the celebration, I had another opportunity to finally stop my administrator from giving me any more bad evaluations. I thought I had won the battle, and life would be great moving forward. I cut one head off, and another one manifested. I was on guard, and my internal dialogue was unhealthy. I was spiritually and physically bankrupt. I was determined to finish the year. I fought to keep my position because I knew my students would feel abandoned, and they needed a consistent teacher. When I saw my hair was falling out in my shower, and I realized my psoriasis had spread all over my body, I knew I needed more time with God and less negative self-talk. By the time I decided to resign, I was under the care of two doctors. At that point, I could hear God loud and clear. I had to stop fighting and stop seeing myself as a victim. I needed to seek professional help. My mind was racing all day. I needed to get my anxiety levels down so I could sleep.

Mental Health

I am an African American certified school counselor K-12, and I am a Licensed Professional Counselor Associate in Texas. I have been a school counselor and a therapist. Yet I did not want to admit I needed a therapist to improve my mental health. I had no idea my feeling of intense, excessive, and persistent worry and fear about everyday situations was anxiety (American Psychiatric Association (APA), 2021). I never learned the actual definition of anxiety until my first appointment with a therapist. Idid not realize my anxiety was interfering with my daily life until my hair went MIA. My body was constantly itching and covered with plaques from psoriasis. According to the APA, anxiety disorders are the most common mental disorders and affect nearly 30% of adults at some point in their lives (APA, 2021). I did not need data to help me understand African American women from low-socioeconomic communities experienced more anxiety than most people in the USA (APA, 2021). Furthermore, I was aware my anxiety disorders affected my job performance, academic work, and personal relationships.

For the strong women, especially African American women reading my book, please allow yourself to admit you cannot do it all alone.I realized talking to friends was not enough. I needed to speak with someone who saw the issues and understood how my mind was fighting its latest trauma. I needed to have a professional who could prescribe the proper medication to help me overcome my fears. I needed someone to tell me it was acceptable to stop fighting.

I admitted I needed medication to help control my anxiety levels. I lost my joy. My Superwoman cape had massive holes in it. I was like Deontay Wilder fighting in the 6th through the 11th rounds against Tyson Fury. I was holding on until the sound of the bell each round. My students could see my weariness. My doctor and my therapist recommended I quit my job. I listened to their expert advice. Then, I went on my medical leave in December 2016. I resigned in January 2017.

I didn't know how taxed I was from working three years at the high school. As a black woman, I was used to pushing past hegemony, verbal abuse, assaults, and disrespect. I was used to experiencing trauma. I was used to absorbing hard blows and dragging myself to the next pitstop to recover and go another round. I usually pushed past the pain and hid it behind a joke or a laugh. I had never faced this type of attack during my 20plus year teaching career.

I recognized that I took too much pride in my evaluations, and I was overwhelmed by the other unfair tactics I dealt with while trying to prove my worth to the new administrators. I did not see this battle as

14

spiritual warfare. I was drained, depressed, distressed, and too angry to consult God during the storm. My beliefs were constantly under attack. I was fighting in my strength with my limited knowledge. I was not sure where my breastplate of righteousness was resting during this battle. My helmet of salvation had a big gash, and the lies I told myself were creeping in my mind all day (Ephesians 6:17). My psoriasis spread over my head, back, legs, and toes.

After leaving the district, my psoriasis became manageable. I also found the right dermatologist. When my hair went MIA, I wore hats to hide my scattered bald spots. I also wore weaves, but I was tired of their weight and maintenance costs. Looking back, I realized I took my beautiful thick hair for granted. I would cut it short and expected it to grow back quickly. After the extreme stress I suffered, my hair thinned out at the top, and it has not grown about thick like it was. I praise God for restoring my hair. I understand the saying, "A woman's hair is her glory," so much better now. My hair is long again, but it took several years of prayer, Humira Pen shots, Taltz pen shots, and a good stylist, O'Neeka Bentley, to get it back on track. Our mental health matters more than high marks on an evaluation and a false appearance of being an excellent teacher.

I realized I had come to terms with how much I fought to maintain my identity as a teacher when it was time to move forward in my career. When I am in public places, people often ask me, "Are you a teacher?" I proudly say, "Yes, I am." Real teachers can be picked out of crowds regardless of their race, sexual orientation, and gender. Our behavior, culture, look, and blood flows with the energy and passion of teachers. When I go to public places like Moody Garden's swim area, children say to me watch me, and they come over and talk with me. If I am in a hall at my children's school, parents will ask me where classes are. I give off the "teacher look/vibe."

For years, I have identified with most teachers' mindsets. I am guilty as most teachers of waiting happily for tiny paychecks because most feel it's their calling to teach. I am guilty, like most teachers, of working side jobs, teaching summer school, and fighting for positions that pay supplement pay to make extra money. Teachers do not leave the profession no matter how much they complain about the profession. We look forward to summer vacations to work our additional job full-time. We love the fact we are off every holiday the bank is closed. Teachers get married and have babies within two-three years into their professions. Teachers give our profession 90 percent of their time, and 20% of our salaries are reinvested into our classes. Teachers dream of retirement. Some more ambitious teachers become school administrators or politicians, like me. I have been doing several things for twenty-plus years, but I primarily identified as a teacher. When I resigned from the district, I did not know who I would be professionally. I knew I would no longer give all my time, money, intellectual property, and energy to anything that I could not make the final decisions on matters that impacted my life professionally, financially, and economically.

I had no idea God was transforming my mindset and identity when I left the district. I could not see myself as a female founder, an executive television producer, or the host of my television show. I did not see myself starting my school, but I saw myself as a Superintendent running an independent school district. I did not know what to do outside of the field of education. Most of my friends were in education. Who would I talk to about my life as an entrepreneur? Most teachers do not leave the professions to start companies; however, they did start side hustles like tutoring businesses. Most of the teachers and professors I knew gave away their successful programs, their researched-based curriculum, and they also stole other educators' intellectual property via the school's copy machine daily. I knew I needed to rest, get my creativity back, and I needed to carve out a new identity for myself before I made any more moves professionally.

To restore my mental health, I worked on loving myself, accepting myself, my flaws, and my failures for five months, while I recouped in my home. I worked on forgiving myself for not being vulnerable enough and not letting go sooner. I had to forgive myself for thinking I was weak for allowing my anxiety to spiral out of control. I started to volunteer because it brought me joy. When I returned from serving in the community, I rested on Orchard Trail Drive in my home. I had time to reflect on all the accomplishments I had achieved while living on Orchard Trail Drive. I have owned my home on Orchard Trail since February 22, 2013. After I finalized the adoption of my three children in 2012, I moved into my home on Orchard Trail. In 2015, I completed my doctorate while living on Orchard Trail. I accomplished a great deal while living in my beautiful 2500 square feet custom-built home in Pearland, TX. My home was my second custom-built home. The house was appraised at $228,000.00.

FIGURE 2 My Home on Closing Day February 22, 2013, Photo by Author

However, I purchased it for $172,695.00. See Figure 2.

Before I transitioned into full- time entrepreneurship, I was a workaholic, and I did not spend a great deal of time resting and enjoying my home. When I was there, I was tired most of the time. I took great pride in being an African American single, via a divorce, mom who lived a pretty good life. Before purchasing my home on Orchard Trail, I had to build my credit before buying my second house.

After I resigned from the school district, I decided to rely on revenue from company as my primary source of income. After my divorce in 2006, I founded my first company, The Resource Center 2007. In the beginning, it was a side hustle, but I started to rethink my vision for myself in 2017. After several honest conversations with myself, I decided I never wanted to have someone else control my destiny or professional reputation. I acknowledged that I lost the ability to sink all my energy into winning at all costs. I did not have the power to fight folks who did not like me and wished to cause mental, financial, or physical harm. When I needed a legal advocate, I would hire one to fight on my behalf. If I needed to avoid, let go, or retreat from someone or something to preserve my peace of mind, I would let go rapidly! In 2016, I hung up my Superwoman cape. When I looked at my hair, I saw the remnants of a battle that almost took me out. I admitted there was no need for any more capes in my life.

While writing this book, Bell Hooks, a black feminist, and renowned author, died on December 15, 2021. I cited her words and thoughts in my dissertation because I identified as a black feminist, and I found her words supported many of my beliefs as a woman. Once again, I found her words supported my view on Black women's mental health.

The number one thing Black women and all Black people should be paying attention to is our health. By that, I mean our physical and mental health because I don't think we can be self-determining without those two strengths. I believe the revolution needs to be self-esteem because we are all assaulted on all sides. It used to be we were attacked by horrendous representations and notions of Blackness coming from White people. Still, now a lot of those notions come to us from Black people (Boone, 2021).

Once I became my boss, I enjoyed my time with my children. My oldest son was 19 at the time, and we had difficulty seeing eye-to-eye. I felt it was time for him live with his father full-time. I knew the moment he moved in with his father; I would lose my income from child support. Allowing him to stay with his father was the best decision I could have made for all of us. Before finalizing my divorce, I spent a lot of time-fighting my ex-husband, over child support. After I resigned from the district, I realized I did not need that fight anymore. He needed his father, and I needed his father to see what I was going through trying to raise him alone. My son helped me so much with his siblings. I did not realize how much I depended on him to watch the children. My son's anger over the boundaries I was setting with him was palatable. I wanted peace with my son too. He did not understand my pain, and I could not understand his pain. His father provided him a safe place to learn about the realities of being an adult without my interventions. I was willing to depart with the money for my peace of mind. I let him go, and I changed my focus to figuring out ways to take care of my family solely with my business' revenues.

Chapter 3

Loving My Upgrades

There were several places within my home where I found the ability to let go of the pressure. Sitting under the arc of my front door calmed me down. I cannot explain why or how the small, enclosed space made me feel so relaxed. After I cut the grass in the front yard, I would sit by the front door and think about how good God was in my life. I would sit down and admire my choices. I loved the style of the bricks and their colors. I liked how the doors, bricks, and shutters looked together. When you customize your home, it is designed by you for you. I spent money on several upgrades because

I realized how much I needed unique items like an oversized tub, a garage with remote control, ceramic tiles throughout the house, and granite countertops to add value to my life. I felt so proud when I watched HGTV and saw my granite pattern. My children would also react when they saw our countertops on television. They would say, "Mom, they have the same countertops." I loved giving out candy every Halloween on Orchard Trail Drive. I loved my landscaping and my door with a glass window. What made me the proudest was that I was one of three single female homeowners on Orchard Trail Drive. When I cut the grass in the front yard, the men on my street would cut their grass too. I was a leader in my subdivision. People trusted me to share their concerns at Homeowners' meetings. I encouraged everyone to protest their appraisals and shared any information I learned from the Neighborhood App. I was elected as a Precinct Chair to represent my district.

My custom master bathroom was my favorite upgrade. The oversized tub helped me accept the extra weight I had put on over the years of raising four children by myself. My master bathroom popped! Again, I saw my creativity every time I walked into my restroom. I selected a high oversized commode seat too. Eventually, I hoped to spend time with a husband in the tub, but that never happened. I had visions of me having a "good time" in the tub with "my husband" when I finally got remarried; I never had the opportunity to marry during the six years I owned my home. I spent hours in my oversized tub soaking without worrying about the water overflowing when I put my thick thighs into it. I did not worry about my legs being so tight I could not move around in the tub. Readers with a little extra weight and height can understand my love for the oversized tub. I spent hours escaping from loud children, planning, thinking, and watching television in my tub.

My kitchen was my other go-to-spots to sit, create, bake, and eat. When I moved into my home Maria, Mercedes, and Maria V. came over and gave me my first set of new dishes. I made so many sacrifices to purchase my home. One of my most significant sacrifices was to

FIGURE 3 The Oversized Island Photo by Author

sell my red convertible Mustang for $3000.00 to buy my stove, refrigerator, and microwave in cash. I had the convertible top redone and added a glass window before I decided to sell it. I still miss my Mustang. I had two other vehicles. The memories of my children laughing and talking in the kitchen were worth me letting go of my car (See Figure 3). I was so glad they bought dishes because I needed them. I needed their friendship after I left Angleton ISD. My mom and sister would come for Thanksgiving and Christmas. I created tons of great memories in the kitchen. I entertained guests in the kitchen, and I danced in the kitchen. I loved my oversized island, and I spent hours sitting around the island. My children grew up right before my eyes while spending time on the island. When I started building my businesses, I completed the paperwork while sitting around the island. God gave me so many creative ideas in the kitchen. When I moved out of my home, I took one more look at my kitchen before I closed the door for the last time. The heart of my house was in the kitchen and living area.

I took pride in my backsplash and all the colors of the kitchen. I used to look at all the newly built homes before the owners moved in to see how they designed their homes. Our homes looked the same outside, but each had unique interior designs. I wish I had purchased a more significant sink and handles for the cabinets. I saw a few kitchens that made me rethink my choices, but I knew the upgrades they purchased were way out of my price points. Some buyers picked all their promotions, and their financing fell through before closing. Therefore, someone else had the opportunity to live in their dream homes with their upgrades. Ironically, someone is enjoying my upgrade too.

Chapter 4

The Quiet Before the Storm

I rented my first office on August 17th, 2017, @ 1415 North Loop W 300-18 in Houston, TX. The pride I felt as an entrepreneur on that day was immense. My dream of becoming a "real business owner" was manifested. I could see a fantastic view of downtown every day and especially at night. I could serve my clients who needed services from the companies I founded in my home on Orchard Trail Drive. If you look at the photo (see Figure11), you can almost see all my teeth in the picture. When I left the district, I withdrew some of my retirement money to sustain me while I regrouped mentally and physically. I decided to invest some of my retirement money to fund my business. I was also excited to do the leg work to secure the space. It is lonely being an entrepreneur. When

FIGURE 4 My First Office Photo by Author

entrepreneurs start, they do everything until they learn better.

For the first time in my career, I committed to betting on myself and my abilities to make money. When I left the school district, I knew I would never be an employee of any district again. Instead, I would become a vendor for the community. My fight was not with the school district; and it was with administrators who worked for the district. I did not have the desire to work full-time at a university. I did not have to rent an office as fast as I did. I could have worked from home for a couple of years. Yet something inside of me pushed me to rent an office space. I learned a little unspoken rule in business that a small business owner needed a stand-alone office and business insurance to be accepted and acknowledged as a business owner.

In 2017, my complete focus was on building a community with other female entrepreneurs and increasing my cliental. I was not dealing with shame as much, but it lurked around, waiting on specific moments of quietness. I was moving from rehearsing what happened to me and thinking about serving others. I was not focusing on my evaluation. At night, I would look out of my office window; I saw God's gift to me. He allowed me to see wealth and possibilities from my small office. I couldnot see God had transformed me into an entrepreneur. My thoughts changed from victim to founder.

I had skin in the game. I was the boss. I was working on my Superintendent certification at UT when I decided to find a school. I wanted to start my school 14 years ago; I could not secure a space. Furthermore, I decided to adopt my first daughter, and I felt I needed to return to work full-time to ensure my daughter. I was disappointed I could not secure a building, and I did not want to adopt a baby without financial security. However, this time, I did not succumb to my internal fears.

On February 21st, 2017, I created my first non-profit in Texas called Dr. Pope's STEM and Liberal Arts Academy. I also secured its 501c3 status. On July 25th, 2017, I received my first Harris County Department of Education (HCDE) Execution of Offer for my school five months later. The contract helped drive my desire to secure office space. I learned securing a contract does not necessarily mean you will get a payout from the agreement. At the beginning of my business journey, I did not ask enough questions, and I did not understand how my contract worked. More importantly, I did not ask enough questions before making a financial commitment to secure the office space. Nevertheless, I was still happy to book an office space.

The TORI Luncheon

I also worked with community leaders to create another non-profit called The Next Move Re-entry Program. It was not my vision, but I was willing to bring it to life. The plan was to handle the paperwork and let another person be the CEO. My fears were driving my decision at the time. I was not used to working with violent ex-offenders. The real reason I want to start a re-entry came from my work at the high school. Many of my students obtained assault cases for fighting. If they fought with a minor, a freshman, they would add another charge to the fighting charge. They might get an endangering or assaulting a minor charge. When students had drugs, they would be charged with a drug case before they reached the age of 18—too many barriers to overcome all the legal issues before they were mature adults. I wanted to end the school-to-prison pipeline. I was never one to just talk about doing things. I acted. I understood creating a non- profit did not mean I expected the company not to make money. Some people love attending meetings, but the real work happens after the sessions. I had to make some tough decisions with this business.

I traveled to Dallas to learn more about TD Jakes' TORI Re-entry program and to see if I could be the face and leader of the program. I wanted to pattern my non-profit like the TD Jakes program. I received confirmation about my leadership at the luncheon. I took a picture with The First Lady, Serita Jakes, and received a copy of his book, "Crushing: God Turns Pressure into Power." Moreover, I met some of the participants enrolled in the TORI program. I learned I could move forward as the face of the non-profit without fear if I focused on my vision and mission for the program. I had to make the program my own.

I did not create its name, but the new mission was mine. I had to let go of my discomfort and fears and move forward. Again, I learned to bet on myself. I knew if I was ready to secure office space, make pitches, recruit clients, and generate revenue for the business, I should be prepared to be the CEO too. I made some difficult choices with friends and community leaders. I learned to be more transparent with everyone about my expectations in partnerships. Again, I learned to get everything in writing and accept when others walk away from the business. In June 2021, I received my first client referral from the TORI Program. I was so glad I followed my gut and traveled to Dallas by myself for the first time.

Eight days after I rented my office space, Hurricane Harvey, a Category 4 storm, hit Texas on August 25th, 2017. I was not ready for Hurricane Harvey and the damage it caused all around my surrounding communities and me. My battle with my identity as an "excellent teacher" was a precursor to the battle I would fight after Hurricane Harvey hit landin Texas.

After the damage Hurricane Harvey did to Texas, lenders were providing homeowners an opportunity to take a reprieve from their mortgage payments. My mortgage lender at the time was Nationstar. I received a call from Nationstar asking if I wanted to participate in a program that would allow me not to pay my mortgage for three months. I told Nationstar that it would delay my mortgage payments for three months. I had just started my business. At the time of the pitch, I had not paid August's mortgage payment at the time of the call. It was August 28th when I received the call from Melissa at Nationstar. I was super excited because I was worried about how I would pay my mortgage.

I quickly said, "Yes!" I felt like God was giving me a break from the pain I had dealt with earlier. I felt like this little reprieve would give me a little nest egg. After all, I lived right and stayed focused on my business. I cried with joy when the call ended. I stayed in Austin, TX for the week, completing an Ex-Offender Certification course for my non-profit. I was going through my retirement money quicker than I had anticipated. When my son lived with his father, I stopped receiving child support. I was adjusting to my new faith walk. Although something inside of me was concerned about the Harvey Program, I pushed past my need for more details and went with my emotions. I called a friend, and we celebrated the blessing.

I purchased my house on February 22nd, 2013. For six years, I was never behind 45 days. I was never in jeopardy of losing my home before Hurricane Harvey. I did whatever I had to do to keep it. I was so proud of how hard I worked to purchase the upgrades. I learned to get what I wanted and felt I needed to enjoy my house and to see my financial investment with my eyes every month. I provided my four children with beautiful rooms. After Hurricane Harvey, the highways to my office were closed due to flooding. I continued to build my business and expand my networks. My bills did not decrease during Harvey. My optimism was extreme, and my faith was strong.

During the months while things were going back to normal after Hurricane Harvey, I started volunteering in the Sunnyside area with the non-profit Peoples United Summit. I also started volunteering with a popular community leader in the Sunnyside community. The community leader advocated for and served senior citizens in Sunnyside. I have always loved serving senior citizens because of my relationship with my Aunt Zeffie Lee Frazier.

My Aunt Zeffie Lee Frazier

I would spend the day with my Aunt Zeffie Lee Frazier while my cousins were in school. We called her Mah. She was my dad's sister. Mah was more like my grandmother. She was a housewife, and she influenced me in so many ways. I learned how to tell time, feed the chickens, read, and eat fruit cake. I also learned to watch "the stories" or soap operas. My Aunt Zeffie Lee Frazier made the best homemade biscuits. When I turned 16, I had another opportunity to spend the summer in Winnfield, Louisiana, with my aunt. I spent a great deal of time with my aunt and Alice. They were around 70. Both dipped Bitter Garett Snuff. My job was to dump the spit jars. My aunt and Alice were smart, independent, and funny women. I enjoyed hanging out with them. While I drove them around Winnfield, I listened to their conversations in the car, fishing, and sitting on the porch. My memories with her were some of the best memories of my life. I have dedicated a considerable part of my life to helping seniors because of my experiences with my Aunt Zeffie Lee Frazier.

My volunteer work with senior citizens in Sunnyside was one of the best things that could have happened to me after Hurricane Harvey because I learned I was being deceived by my mortgage company. The popular community leader assigned me a few seniors to assist, completing my Licensed Professional Counselor Associate's hours. I loved helping them, so it was a great opportunity. There were stipulations I had to adhere to while volunteering. The stipulations were never to take money from the seniors, never harm them, and never take advantage of them. I went to work with three ladies immediately.

I was assigned to help Sweetie keep her home. I discovered she was in a Hurricane Harvey program too. Sweetie's mortgage lender was Wells Fargo Bank. Sweetie was scared she was going to lose her home. When I got involved with Sweetie's case, I learned Wells Fargo posted all their transactions and communication with their homeowners online. They communicated with Sweetie via the telephone, and they sent her emails. I was added to her email account to share with them on her behalf. She was asked to complete any paperwork on Wells Fargo's online portal. I could download the forms, and we made sure we followed directions. I was able to speak with the representative from Wells Fargo on speakerphone along with Sweetie. I had no idea God was using my willingness to help Sweetie fight her battle as a way of preparing me for my struggle with Nationstar.

I was assigned two other ladies that did not need help with their mortgage paperwork. Instead, I helped them with their medication needs, secured a wheelchair, secured a unique bed, and completed paperwork for insurance coverage. I completed Sweetie's Well Fargo Harvey Program paperwork. I gave a great deal of my time serving in Sunnyside while I waited to see what was happening with my own home. I kept a good attitude because I could move around and network. I was beginning to generate some business with a few non-profits. I obtained their 501c3 status. I also designed websites. I was earning money while I served in the community. Although I could see my mindset was changing. More importantly, I started to see myself as a businesswoman.

I did not tell anyone I was beginning to feel uneasy about the status of my home. I had not heard anything regarding my mortgage or the program from Nationstar Mortgage from September 2017-October 2017. In November 2017, I received a letter from Nationstar Mortgage stating my mortgage was sold to Mr. Cooper Mortgage Company. I immediately questioned if Mr. Cooper was honoring Nationstar's Harvey Program. I had not received any paperwork regarding the program. I was so grateful not to have to pay the mortgage, and it freed up money to tackle my other debts. Later, I would learn Mr. Cooper Mortgage was the new name of Nationstar Mortgage. Nationstar was <u>sued, so they changed their name and </u>launched a new branding campaign.

By November 2017, I realized I needed to downsize to make my retirement money stretch. I was eliminating expensive car payments. I was generating some revenue, but I was having trouble collecting money from clients. I became more aware that something was not right with the mortgage company. I started ramping up my calls to Nationstar DBA Mr. Cooper Mortgage Company. The representative would tell me, "Oh, you know what, don't worry about it. Everything's okay?" When I would speak with Melissa, the representative who initially told me about the program, she would say, "Okay. Don't worry about it." Then, in January 2018, the trap was sprung. I was made aware of an application I needed to complete, but it was not ready. I asked, "What application? Where do I get the application?" I had to apply for the program for the first time. I asked several representatives, "Why would I need to apply for the program I was previously enrolled in since August 2017?"

Meanwhile, I was receiving calls from the mortgage company to see the property's condition. Then, I noticed people were coming to check on the property physically. I was unaware of when their representatives would visit. When I asked the representatives about the people walking around my front yard and the gold notes on my door, they said the people were checking in and inspecting the house. Thank God I helped Sweetie with her mortgage paperwork. I learned Mr. Copper was not being transparent in their dealings with me. I demanded to be able to see my account status online. I told the representatives I knew I would receive information about my account balance. Seven months went by before I could finally see my account balance. I owed $15,000 in back mortgage payments. I was terrified at this point. Deep down, I was banking on the fact they would move the $15,000.00 to the end of the balance of my mortgage. It should have been a simple transaction. I had gotten behind on my car payment in the past, and they took two car payments and moved them to the end of the loan. Once I made the payment arrangement, I assumed the Harvey Program was the same.

Finally, on January 20th, 2018, I downloaded an application from Mr. Cooper's website. I also learned the program's name was the Home Affordable Modification Program. The application was simple on the surface, and I discovered the program was a remodification program. I downloaded a Profit and Loss statement along with the application, and I asked the representative.

The Profit and Loss Statement seemed as if I was refinancing my home. None of it made sense to me, and it did not make sense that I had to keep resubmitting the same documents. I realized Mr. Cooper was wasting my time and burying me in redundant emails. I demanded Mr. Cooper provide me with a way to indicate they received my paperwork immediately.

My anxiety levels started to increase again, and I started worrying about losing my hair again. While I was rebounding from the battle with the school district, I developed a plan to keep my hair on my head. I made sure I maintained my medication for my psoriasis. My mindset was different during this fight. I told God I would sell my home before losing my mind or hair. I lost faith in people and the system. Mr. Cooper required me to fill out one Profit and Loss statement five times. They asked for my business address, but there was no place for it, so I wrote it on top of the form. I had to correct the paper. One representative said they received my paperwork on the phone. Yet, I would receive a letter requesting the same form again via traditional mail. I was sending emails to several representatives. The more I demanded to receive a receipt via email; they would switch the representative. I was assigned one representative that Mr. Cooper claimed was out due to health issues. They claimed they could not retrieve her emails while she was out. Everything the mortgage company told me was via verbal communication. I had no proof of anything on my end. After filling out the Profit and Loss statement, representatives assuredme that everything was okay.

In March 2018, I received the awful news that I did not qualify for the program. The information was a shock. Ironically, I did not qualify for the program because I was late with my August 2017 mortgage payment. Hurricane Harvey hit Texas on August 25th, 2017, and Melissa from Nationstar called me on August 28th, 2017. I clearly remembered I accepted the program offered via the phone three days after Harvey. I tried to figure out Nationstar's realistic plan for its customers impacted by the hurricane. In May, I was sending emails to Mr. Cooper explaining my frustration with their system.

After being crushed by the knowledge that I failed to qualify for the Home Affordable Modification Program, the mortgage company announced they had sent me the wrong paperwork. They said they would fix their error by sending me the correct paperwork for their "other" program. I continued to submit paperwork via email to different dedicated loan specialists, and I was tired of the electronic email system. I spent hours on the phone with various representatives. One of the representativeswould leave a message for one month, but she would never return my calls or send an email stating what she needed.

Meanwhile, men continued to come to the house to check on the property. They never entered my home or spoke directly with me. Nine months into the process, I received a Notice of Substitute Trustee's Sale from RAS Crane, LLC, dated May 23rd, 2018. According to the letter, the auction would take place on August 07th, 2018.

I was dumbfounded because I could not understand how I went from being enrolled in a program supposedly created to help those impacted by Hurricane Harvey to being embroiled in a nightmare to save my home from my lender, Mr. Cooper. I called Mr. Cooper when I received the Deed of Trust Certified Letter. I was angry, perplexed, and embarrassed because they not only sent me the letter, but they also sent it to my Homeowners Association. I just happened to be serving as a Board Member at the time. I was the only African American too. In my humiliation, this time, my legal mind kicked into gear. I am not a lawyer, but I think critically. My analytical side finally kicked into play during this battle. I was afraid, but I knew all of this made no sense. I was on my medication, so my anxiety levels were normal. I was sleeping and thinking clearly. I was not angry to the point of no return. Believe it or not, I was a pre-law major when I started at the University of Houston-Downtown.

I understood a scam on paper, and I was mad at myself because it took me so long to figure it out. It was a farce. Mr. Cooper presented their customers, who Hurricane Harvey impacted, an opportunity for a reprieve on their mortgage payments for three months. Still, that reprieve was an opportunity for the mortgage company to steal people's properties legally. They held the application for six months so the homeowners' mortgage payments would default. I could have made a payment, but representatives told me that it was unnecessary. I knew Wells Fargo was handling their program distinctly differently.

My battle with shame and hubris struck again! I did not go to Legal Aid. I made my biggest mistake by not securing an attorney during the process. I saw how Legal Aid handled Sweetie's case, and I was not impressed. I did not think I needed one. Plus, the cost of securing an attorney was a significant factor in my decision. I was embarrassed, and I did not want people to know. I thought about the equity I had in my home, and I realized my mortgage company would drain my equity. I had about $62,000 in equity. If I had sold my home for the appraised value of $228,000.00, I could have walked away from the table feeling good and with a bit of nest egg. I did not have peace with the idea of moving. I was mentally drained. I was falling in love with being home and creating my businesses.

To this day, I still do not understand why I did not attempt to sell my home! It was the obvious solution. Once again, I believed God would provide a solution. Again, I trusted my intellect to help me figure out a realistic solution. Finally, my account was accessible online. I called the mortgage company, and they said the letter from RAS Crane was a mistake. They assured me they were not taking me home. They said I received the letter because "they" did not see I was under the Homebuyer Program. The representative said they were going to get me the correct paperwork. I called RAS Crane, LLC, and they said they did not have the house for sale. However, I had the paperwork. I talked with so many representatives, and they all said the Deed of Trust Sale was an error.

Eventually, I spoke with a wise representative who found the problem with my account. He talked with me for over two hours on the phone. He said he figured out what happened to my application and what caused the trouble. He explained there were two types of remodification programs. Somehow, my account was not appropriately labeled. My loan was treated as a traditional remodification. The representative assured me that he would direct me to the right person and resolve the issue. Later, a representative named James told me he had the solution. He said they had processed my paperwork like a traditional modification. The remodification was under the Harvey Program. He said, "We realized we dropped the ball." He said they were "going to fix it." He said I would get some paperwork saying that you would pay this payment. Then, if you do not make the payment, you know you will be in trouble. The representativereiterated that if I missed the payment, Mr. Cooper planned to take me home. I knew in my gut Mr. Cooper would foreclose on my house regardless of my payment. They were supposed to put the $15,000.00 money in arrears at the end of my loan. There was no need to threaten to take my home. I continued to wonder why I was about to lose my home after Mr. Cooper admitted they dropped the ball. I received information from Mr. Cooper's Disaster Relief Team requesting proof of my hardship. Hurricane Harvey was the reason for the program.

I made mistakes too. The first mistake was not making my mortgage payments after three months passed. Although the representatives told me not to make the payments because everything was fine, I knew I should have made my payments. By the time I was aware of the $15,000.00 balance, I should have contacted an attorney. I could not see how they calculated $15,000.00 on a six-month mortgage payment of $1490. I would have owed $8,940.00 (not including any late fees). I continued to hope they were going to keep their words.

I spoke with James, a Mr. Cooper representative, in November of 2018. James assured me I was not going to lose my home. He also said I did not need to make a payment. They were not going to take a partial payment at that time on a $15,000.00 balance. They were supposed to take the amount due and put it at the end of the mortgage. I was still dealing with a pending condition that I would lose my home if I did not make the payment on a specific date listed on the correct paperwork. I received the paperwork that stated I needed to make the payment in January 2019. I signed the paperwork and continued to feel uneasy, but I trusted the process. By then, my retirement money was gone. I was not worried because I knew I would have a tax refund in February. I also knew I had money coming in January to pay the mortgage.

Chapter 5

The Community Leader

On January 19th, 2019, I turned 50. I felt I was ready to serve in Pearland on another level. I decided to run for Pearland City Council. I had been serving as a Democratic Precinct Chair in Brazoria County. I was a delegate for SD 11 for several years. I worked with local Democrats for over ten years. I was on my HOA Board. I have always volunteered in some form or fashion since my high school days on Student Council. I did not have any money to purchase signs, but I felt good about my decision to run because of an interview I had a year earlier with State Representative Shawn Thierry, Dist. 146.

I became a Community Television Producer at Houston Media Source in August 2018. Again, while I was rebounding from the battle with the school district, I was volunteering in Sunnyside. My service in Sunnyside presented another opportunity to evolve into someone I never dreamed of becoming. The popular community leader in Sunnyside invited me to accompany her on Bishop Delagraentiss' television show at Houston Media Source. When I walked into the studio, I immediately realized I was supposed to be on television. I was so comfortable with the technology, and I loved the entire process. Within two months, I was a Community Producer. I had my television show called "Conversations with Dr. Pope." My show aired on AT&T U-Verse channel 99 and Comcast 17.

I realized God was maneuvering me during this entire process. After a year, I filmed and produced my first television show in the district I had previously left. This whole process was part of my restoration with the school district. I filmed my first television show at the same High School I had resigned from a year prior. God had brought me full circle. The first person I interviewed was State Representative Shawn Thierry (District 146). During our conversation, she referred to me as a Community Leader. It was the first time I identified as a labeled Community Leader. Instantly, on August 18th, 2018, I saw myself as a Community Leader. I loved the label because it fit what I did most of my life. I wouldn't say I liked the term politician because of its negative connotation. However, I loved the term Community Leader. It fit my essence and my mission in life. Once I was accepted the label, I was a Community Leader; I saw the possibilities of becoming a Pearland City Councilwoman.

In January 2019, I launched my campaign for Pearland City Council. I focused on helping the small business owners keep and grow their businesses, connecting the different regions (communities) within Pearland, and representing female voices in the city of Pearland. At the time, we did not and still do not have any women serving on Pearland's City Council. By the time I launched my campaign, I had embraced my new identity as a Community Leader and businesswoman. I moved forward in my campaign to learn all I could about my community and its small business owners. Brazoria County is a Republican County. I attended meetings with some welcoming Republicans. I went to every invite, and I took my children with me so they could see me do the work. I found we had more in common than different. I was nervous about the debate because I waited for someone to ask me about my secret. If they knew, they did not bring it up.

I learned Pearland has some strong women helping men get elected. I wish those powerful women would put some energy into getting a woman regardless of her race, sexual orientation, and the political party elected to serve on the council. We have had three women elected to help so far. Sometimes, I was the only open Democrat at a function, but I did my best to show everyone a woman could make an argument and serve everyone in the city. My opponent won the election fairly. My numbers were higher than other Democrats who ran for Pearland City Council. I did not have any money to purchase signs, but people knew who I was. I am still a community leader and an elected official. I am a Democratic PrecinctChair for Precinct 46. I am not sure if I would run again for City Council. I learned the meetings were long and a little dry. Maybe a woman would move things a little faster and cut out some posturing.

I was supposed to make my payment in January 2019. I was not worried about making the payment in January because I had a contract witha local non-profit to help with their annual fundraiser. I was hired to provide social media services for the annual fundraiser. I knew the Vice President of the non-profit because I had worked with him for over ten years in another political organization. He knew me when I only had my son. He had always talked to my son at our meetings. I thought he was a good role model. Then, he watched me adopt three other children and pack them to our political events. I thought he hired me to allow me to showcase my media company and help my family. This fundraiser contract would be an additional income stream for me in January. I had a monthly direct deposit coming to pay my mortgage every month. It did not pay for other expenses.

When I talked with the organization leaders about my contract as a Social Media Manager for their fundraiser, I insisted I receive my payment upfront. I immediately noticed he was trying to low-ball my prices by claiming not to have money to pay the fee I was asking for my services, and I was not charging too much money. The group insisted I meet with them during their planning meetings. I said I did not need to meet with them, but they made it part of the deal. I did not charge them for their meeting times. Again, I was trying to figure out how to earn money and build my business.

As time progressed, I told the leaders they needed a better website. To allow customers to register for the fundraiser, they need links to accept payments. I added videos and other items to make the website look professional and promote the event's theme. One of the leaders asked me to do the work. They had meetings and discussed the need for the website. Finally, they agreed they needed one, and I should create it. Here is where I made a huge mistake. I decided to build the website, but I did not give them the cost verbally or in writing until I designed it. They did not know what they needed, and I needed to create something to get moving with their timeline. During a conversation with one of the group leaders, I told them my websites start at $1500.00. Moving forward, they knew the minimum cost for their website was $1500.00. Again, I was sitting on phone calls with the non-profit's leadership discussing the website. They start to demand I join their organization. They could see I was adding value to their team. I did not like their approach, so I refused to join their organization. They insisted on making joining their organization a condition of paying me. I declined to join them, and they agreed to pay me to build their website.

In two days, I built a beautiful $3000.00 website. Other website designers would have charged them more, not managed the website, and not been on call 24-seven. I did the work to build their website to meet the organization's need to sell tickets, receive donations, and promote their event. I took on the role of the website manager. In that role, I made sure everything worked properly. I saw the money they were raising and the donations they were generating. After I built the website, the Vice President constantly called me to make changes and add more features. I reminded him that he had not paid for my work, and he did not pay for 24- hour maintenance of the website. He said, "Do not worry, I got you." I made the changes he requested. They made over $11,000.00 in November and early part of December. I did not know how much money they had on hand before the fundraiser.

The leaders of the organization said they loved the website. I assumed they would pay for the website they claimed brought them such joy. My website was a vast difference from their original website. I never took down their actual website; I used their domain name to direct traffic to their new website. On the night of their event, the President asked me how much I was charging them for the website. I told the President my fee was $3000. I had fun and worked hard, and I expected to get my funds ASAP. They had the cash on hand.

After the event was over in December 2018, I reached out to the leaders of the non-profit regarding my payment. I did not send an invoice. However, I had several phone calls, emails, and text conversations regarding my payment. If I had not known two of the people in the non-profit, I would have handled things differently. Before building the website, I let my need to avoid rippling the water cloud my gut instinct to ask for my payment before I built the website. More important, I would not have spent part of the mortgage money I had in my account on another bill. I risked my guaranteed money on a verbal promise and money I saw entering their account. After this mess ended, I realized that I had to own my part in the debacle to move forward. At this point, I was angry at myself for my judgment issues. I asked about my payment several times before I started to panic and took things into my own hands.

While I was looking for a solution, I remembered another website I designed for a community organization, a non-profit, that refused to pay me for almost two months. My answer then was to take their website offline. I sent a message to my contact person to let them know it was down. I told them it would stay offline until they paid me. When they realized it was down, they paid me quickly. I hoped this non-profit would do the same thing if I took their website offline. I mistakenly thought they would pay me out of the funds they had on hand. I told the same gentlemen who asked me to build the website I would take the website offline until they paid me. He said he was going to take care of it. However, he was unsuccessful. I proceeded to speak with the Vice President because I knew his wife was the Treasurer, so I knew he had the power to make it happen. Instead of getting me a payment, he said I needed to wait until they paid the hotel. Two weeks later, I approached him, and he told me, "He would give me a love offering for my work." I had all kinds of concerns about his "LOVE offering," but I did not respond. I wish I could say he was the only community leader who used God as a hustle, but he is not. I learned working with some church folks, and community leaders can be perplexingand disheartening.

After some time, I took my concerns to the organization's President. He, too, made promises. I spent almost two hours talking with this man and listening to him discuss his integrity and how he would not harm my family. However, by the end of December, I was not paid. Nor was I paid by January 15th. I never received payment from the organization. I could have taken the website offline during their fundraiser, but I felt that was not the best way to solve my problem. I wanted to bepaid not to disrupt their fundraiser or business.

I waited until the event was over. I still had access to the organization's accounts. They had their money, and I needed my money. The website I built had served its purpose; therefore, I took it offline and replaced their domain with their original website. If any of their web trafficor members wanted to go to their website, they would be directed to their original one. I told the organization leaders that if they wished to utilize the website I designed, they needed to pay for it. The Vice President was angry. He threatened to embarrass me during my campaign, but he did not offer to pay me. The President said because I took the website offline, they did not owe me the money. They had no idea, nor did they care how much I depended on that $3000.00. If the leaders had offered $1500.00, I would have walked away happy. They looked at me and saw a transaction. They did not care about my time, home, children, reputation, or business. They had made their money, and I made them look great. It's incredible how clients want business owners to wait for their money, but clients cannot wait for their services.

Due to my false hope in the leadership of the non-profit, I spent themoney I originally had for my mortgage. I risked the money I had in my possession for an expectation that never happened. I had other debts that I needed to take care of, and I made the call to trust my assessment of the organization's leadership. I also saw the money the organization raised through its fundraiser. The leaders told me they would pay me. It's hard to accept blame for this foolishness, but to rebound, I had to admit my part in my downfall, and I had to forgive myself for my part.

When I accepted the gravity of my decisions in January 2019, I realized so much about myself as a Christian, a community leader, a woman, and a businesswoman had transformed into a completely new person. I accepted I could make a risky decision, which caused me to fail tomake the most critical mortgage payment in the six years of owning my home. I gave the ammunition for Mr. Cooper to justify their course ofaction. I came to terms with the following lessons I learned:

1. Never spend money before it's tangible and in your possessions.

2. The missed mortgage payment was not the end of my life; it was the leverage the bank needed to follow through with its original plan.

3. People will refuse to pay you regardless of receiving an invoice, having cash on hand, and regardless of their strong protest, to be honest. In the words of Shakespeare, "The lady doth protest too much methinks" (3.2-210-219).

4. NEVER perform a service without getting all the details and expectations in writing and always collect payments upfront.

5. When clients try to bully you or claim your prices are too high duringnegotiation, sever ties quickly.

6. People will treat you like a transaction or an opportunity to improve theirsocial and financial standings.

7. People should treat church and community leaders the same way theytreat other businesses. Get payments upfront.

8. When clients refuse to pay you after 30-90 days, listen to God handlethem. Get an attorney if necessary.

9. When church, community, and business leaders show you who they areat their core, believe them and act accordingly.

Let God show you how to use your pain to push you to your next level.

At this point, I want to share I never spoke to any of the members of the non-profit after this incident took place. When people try to rebound from a mishap, some need closure to move forward, help them forgive themselves for their role, and forgive others who played a role in their pain. In October of 2019, the President of the non-profit organization saw my post about an event at the Houston Food Bank on Facebook. He called me to verify his assumptions of why I needed help from the Houston Food Bank. The arrogance this community leader had was unimaginable. I was shocked he called. Then, I realized he was still following me on social media. His call reminded me my enemies were always watching me. More importantly, I learned God dealt with my enemies even when I thought they had gotten away with hurting my family and my business.

I answered his call and told him I was at the Houston Food Bank because I was in the process of rebuilding my life after losing my home due to his refusal to pay me. He immediately defended his decision not to pay me, but I knew God was behind the call. I believe he felt convicted. He tried to say he was taken aback by my tone. Users always want to blame those they misuse. Users expect a pass on their harmful behavior. I handled him like a person who had stolen from me. I felt he was mighty arrogant and disrespectful to call and demand verification about my post. Maybe the posts triggered or pricked his conscience. I did not let him off the hook. He needed to see a consequence for his entire teams' refusal to pay me. I explained the Houston Food Bank had a Halloween event, and our intention for going to the food bank was to get food so we could eat for the month and Thanksgiving. I did not let him slide.

I was respectful when I answered his call and shared my rationale for using the Houston Food Bank. I had released my shame when I posted about the new program the Houston Food Bank offered for working people who needed assistance. I was letting other women like myself know about a valuable resource. My Facebook followers needed to know I was not a volunteer at the Food Bank. I was there because I needed community resources. I was a single mother trying to feed her three children without food stamps and a steady income. I needed to share that information with him for closure for me. God allowed me to have one last word with him without me showing up on his doorstep. It did not cross my mind to ask him for my money. I did not need to explain my choices to him, but God needed him to hear the outcome of his refusal to use the very donations he asked the community to give him to help others. I was needy, but I was willing to work. My payment was not an offering or donation. It was my wage for building their organization's website. He has never called again.

I questioned what was happening in my life after I did not makethe payment to Mr. Cooper in January 2019 as promised. I did not lose my faith in God. I was praying and listening to several pastors. I constantly listened to God and went to church until COVID-19 shut it down. When I would sit quietly, questions inundated me. Some of my friends asked why I didn't get a loan to make the payment. I could have gotten a personal loan or the deadly Payday loan. I did not know if I would have the funds to pay the loan because I had just started the business.

Moreover, I escaped the clutches of the Payday Loan trap years ago. I promised myself I would never get another PAY for a LIFE Loan. Once someone travels down the road to Pay Day Loans, they can rarely get off the rollercoaster. I could have asked a friend for a loan, but something deep inside said I should not lose my home over the January payment. I was not ready to tell people my business, and I felt I might be self-sabotaging my business. I repeatedly revisited why I did not attempt to sell my home before January. One of the biggest questions I had was why I didn't save money over the year.

I knew most of the answers to my questions. I had high debt and a small revenue generated from my business. I also had several unexpected expenses. I beat myself up over not having money for a rainy day. I had downsized my cars, and I realized walking by faith took more than I imagined. I owned a Mercedes that was free and clear. The transmission was going out. It gave me the blues, and I was pouring money into it. Two different mechanics told me not to get it repaired anymore. It became an asset to use for a loan.

I also had a Traverse that had a high car note. I called the finance company and said come pick it up. I had excellent payment history. They were willing to work with me, but I knew I could not make the payments anymore. I did not have my child support payment anymore. I wanted to keep my office and my home. I moved out of my business space at the end of my lease. I missed my office, but I knew I had to accept a new way of life. I was no longer making my salary, and my retirement money was almost gone.

Although I feared losing my home, I was relieved they said I did not pay the mortgage. At the time, I didn't see not paying my mortgage for a year as a blessing. When I bought my home, I made an excellent salary and had multiple income streams. When I left the school district and started my business, I downsized to survive. Hurricane Harvey negatively impacted my business, but I continued to focus on mental and physical health. I was experiencing so much trauma back-to-back. I thought my home was the place I would rebuild and decrease my stress levels. Keeping my home was adding stress to my life. My businesses were constantly creating challenges, and I questioned if I needed to return to full-time employment.

Moreover, I started to see the money owed from the website as a reason for my economic troubles. When people become desperate, they look for something to alleviate their fears. In my desperation, I began to question if I was forceful or aggressive enough with the leadership of the non-profit to get the money to solve my problem. From 10 to around 16, I lived in low-income housing apartments in Louisiana. Fighting mentally and physically to protect yourself came with living the environment. I was an only child, so I had to back up whatever I said or did. I said and did plenty. I was my protector. If someone owed me money, I would aggressively collect it. I ran my store. I sold candy. Some of my classmates did not always want to pay for the candy they asked for on credit. I never feared going to someone's house to collect a debt. I never feared the consequences of standing up for myself from bullies or my enemies.

My old instincts to collect my money were desperately trying to return. God had to remind me I could never use any tactics to negate his teachings. I refused to do anything that would tarnish my witness. He reminded me He was and would always be my provider. He promised me He would continue to care for my children and me if I let Him fight my battles. When I adopted three of my four children, I never saw this in my vision. I thought about calling and demanding the leader who asked me to build the website to pay me out of his pocket and seek reimbursement from the organization. I had to let my plan and thoughts go! It was the same voice I heard when I was trying to stay at the high school past my allotted time. I recognized the voice, and I quickly obeyed it.

I was overwhelmed with fear of my consequences for missing the January 30th, 2019, payment. One day I realized my hairline was growing back. Finally, my body was not covered in plaques from my psoriasis. I knew I had to contact the mortgage company. I prayed and made the call to the mortgage company. I asked the representative could they move my payment date to February 8th, 2019. They refused. I surrendered any thoughts I had about trying to collect the payment. I learned to trust my inner voice and the word of God.

Trusting God does not mean I was not angry with my lender, Mr. Cooper. They had me in a difficult spot. They knew they had planned to steal my home, and I had just given them the combination to the safe. I knew losing my home because of Mr. Cooper's mistakes was not legal. Suddenly, after I hung up the phone, I realized people would learn I would have my house foreclosed on while I was running for Pearland City Council. I just sat in my bed and waited for my anxiety to calm down while I determined what was going to be my next move.

I told the representative I would make both payments on February 8th, 2019. I had a direct deposit and my income tax refund to pay the mortgage. The representative called and said I just needed to complete another set of papers. I finished the paperwork in February. They called and told me I needed to complete more paperwork, and I finished them and emailed them as usual. I was in communication with Mr. Cooper from February through April.

I can say with peace of mind that I did what I needed to do with the non-profit organization's leadership. I finally accepted that I had to transition from blaming to devising a plan to move forward. I had to forgive myself and push ahead. I needed to focus on a solution and not see myself as a victim. I was not a victim; I took a calculated risk. It failed. My return on my investment (ROI) with the organization was negative, but there was an upside. I was set free from having to deal with any of them anymore. They would no longer call me to see if I would join their organization or help them. They would not have access to my influence. They would avoid me at all costs. I would not have to entertain false smiles and fake conversations. Suddenly, I realized God permanently broke my connection to them.

Chapter 6

The Note on the Door

By June 2019, I was receiving calls and letters from other realtors. Several realtors were sending me letters about foreclosing on my home. People were always parked outside my house asking to speak with me. Some were rude. Some realtors invaded my privacy. Sometimes I would receive group texts about selling my home. I was always scared someone I knew would approach me and my secret would be public. Some of the realtors were like vultures. I was humiliated and embarrassed. I had made it through the campaign with my secret intact. During my campaign, I learned so much about Pearland and small business owners in Pearland. I did not win, but I felt good about my effort. I pushed myself to do something I never saw myself doing at a time in my life where I understood why it was essential to have a say in local government.

Being a homeowner is vital, and homeowners need more laws to protect them from losing their property to mortgage companies and Homeowners Associations (HOA). I learned small businesses need more ways to collect their payments outside of lawsuits. Small companies in Pearland open and close quickly. I was fighting to keep my business afloat and to save my home. I also spoke about the City of Pearland's water issue.I was making payments on my $600 water bill. Ironically, the City of Pearland is currently trying to figure out why homeowners received high water bills. I talked about Pearland's water issues during the Pearland Chamber debate in May 2019. In 2020, Pearland started to address the extreme water bills residents received.

By June 2019, I seriously thought about moving and selling my home. The thought raised my anxiety levels. I have a doctorate (Ph.D.), and I am a scholar, but I failed to research my lender, Mr. Cooper. I cannot tell you why I did not sit down and Google them earlier. However, I had started to contact government agencies to file a complaint against Mr. Cooper. I started doing my due diligence to learn who I was fighting mentally. A little girl from Louisiana began to emerge again. This time, I was directing my energy to Mr. Cooper. I also admitted I did not want to continue to fight to pay my mortgage monthly. I had to do more to generate more revenue. I knew I had to do something, but I did not have a plan in place. I found several articles regarding Nationstar Mortgage DBA Mr. Cooper during my research. Please click on the following links to readeach article:

- Nationstar Mortgage Returning $86M to Homeowners

- Nationstar Mortgage to refund $73M to borrowers under order

- Mr. Cooper settles $90M lawsuit over illegal foreclosures

- Unauthorized Mortgage Payments

- DFPI Joins $88 Million Multi-State Settlement with NationstarMortgage

- <u>You Can Change a Troubled Company's name, but Its TroublesDon't Go Away</u>

An article in the *Washington Post* by Michelle Singletary (2020) echoed almost precisely what happened to me during my loan modification process. The CFPB complaint, filed in federal district court in D.C., said Nationstar failed to identify requests for loan modifications, which are supposed to help borrowers with their payments. The company allegedly foreclosed while some homeowners were still waiting for their loan modification applications to be processed even though Nationstar had promised it would not do so.

Mr. Cooper made promises not to foreclose on my home, and they lied. My house was foreclosed on in an accelerated timeline while completing the applications. I never received any certified paperwork from a title company notifying me of the new Deed of Trust sale. Meanwhile, I thought I was completing a new application. Nationstar DBA Mr. Cooper has a history and a pattern of stealing their homeowners' property. The title companies seem to play a role in these white-collar crimes. Homeowners do not have any natural protection or rights. How can so many states have lawsuits against Nationstar DBA Mr. Cooper, and the mortgage industry does not shut them down?

On June 6, I was lying down in my room, exhausted. My children came into my room and said, "A lady left this letter in the door." I opened it. The letter stated my house on Orchard Trail Drive had been foreclosed on and sold on June 4, 2019. I never received any certified paperwork stating Deed of Trust Sale would auction off my home in June 2019. Immediately I called Mr. Cooper. At first, the representative claimed they did not sell my home. Then, she put me on hold. She confirmed they had sold it for failure to make payments when she returned. I started to scream at the woman on the phone. I did not know what to do. I continued to ask her how this could happen. I wanted to know what happened with the new paperwork. I hung up the phone, and I started to walk in circles in my bedroom. My heart was beating fast, and I was scared. I was panicked, and my anxiety was kicking into high gear.

While walking in circles in my bedroom, I asked how the representative sold my home. Ironically, my house was auctioned off when my publishing company was publishing its first book. They held the auction on June 4, 2019. On June 5, 2019, Pope's Resource Center, LLC published its first eBook. I danced and celebrated a year of my time creating, editing, and coaching my author to the finish line. During a year filled with such stress, I was able to help create an eBook on Amazon. I had worked on this project with my client and author, Raven Moore, EdD, for a year.

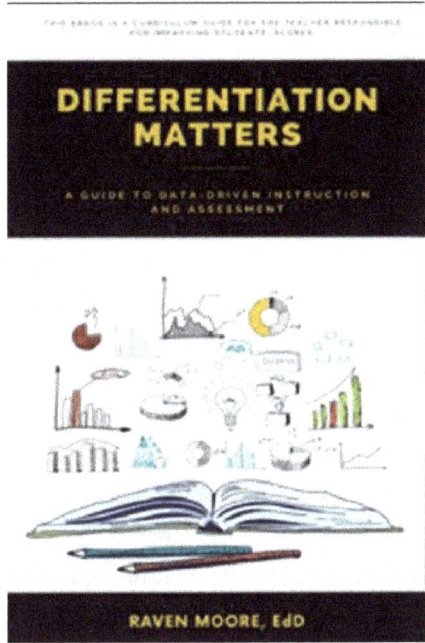

FIGURE 5. First Published Book by Raven Moore, EdD

The year I was running for office, fighting off the wolves, and coming to terms with selling my home, my nightmare occurred. On June 6, 2019, my joy turned to disbelief and utter shock. As I focused on being a creator, God had answered my prayer. I wanted to know what I was supposed to do next. A year of fear ended with a letter telling me this fight was over on my door. According to the letter I had to move in one week. I noticed there were errors with their timeline. My mind was suddenly sharp enough to see loopholes I could use to fight a little longer. I put my head on a pillow and screamed several times. When I stopped screaming, I got up and called my sister. I did not cry. I sought refuge on my patio. I could fall sleep quickly on mypatio couch.

Immediately, I fell back on old behaviors. I started to worry about what people were going to think. I was running for City Council, and my house was not in order. I was humiliated and thinking about how lenders and creditors will re-evaluate me. When I called my sister to tell her about the letter, she said to take the note seriously and get an attorney. She told me to get a storage unit with a free moving truck. I listened and tried to wrap my head around the fact that I had to move within a week. She told me where to get boxes. When I moved into my home six years earlier, I used professional movers for most of my moves. I did not have a great deal of money. Luckily, I secured a new dissertation client, so I had some money.

I was invited to two events before the auction. When I decided to continue with my plans, I was shocked to hear the first presenter share their experience with an eviction. I felt the need to jump out of my seat and run to my car. His story hit close to home. I kept it together and thanked God for letting me hear his story. He appeared to have no shame when he shared his story. I did not share my predicament with him once we spoke. Then, I attended the Pearland Chamber of Commerce's Business Luncheon. I was excited to hear from the CEO and founder of Gringos. I was surprised to learn he lost his home to foreclosure and had his car repossessed before Gringos made him a millionaire. I was encouraged and in tears. I felt like God was trying his best to let me know I would survive this moment. One of my favorite scriptures is, "And this too shall pass." (2 Corinthians 4:17-18). I needed to hear both speakers share their experiences and how they overcame them.

I reached out to the exact real estate attorney I used when I had issues with my office space, Mr. Howard. He was worth every dollar I paid him. Sometimes you need an advocate when you cannot fight anymore. I was embarrassed, but I told him what had happened. I gave him all the documentation, so he could see what I could not see or understand. He asked me to give him some time, and he was going to investigate. He told me how much it would cost, and it did not matter because I needed him.

The letter moved me into action. My lawyer said I should have reached out to him earlier. He said there wasn't much that he could do. He told me how much it would cost to get the house back. I needed at least $3000 to start a long fight to get the house back. He was clear about my options. I found out later during the process, once a person's home was foreclosed, it was tough to get it back. So, I felt the idea of getting my house back was unrealistic. I needed more time to move. I needed more money to pay him and to move. I left his office with a plan and a little of my dignity. His mission was to get me more time in the house and to help me avoid an eviction. I agreed to pay him $1000.00 to get started. Making the payment hurt, but it was necessary. I did not want to have an eviction on my record. I could not pack up a four-bedroom home in one week. I learned earlier when I dealt with Mr. Howard that he would do what I wanted him to do. I knew what I wanted him to do, and I was willing to pay for it.

My lawyer told me I did well, considering I was a layman. He said I did an excellent job holding them off for a year. He could see they had a plan to take me home earlier, and the project was for May 2018. His assessment made me realize I had not wasted all my time and energy over the last year. My attorney made me feel like I would help other people, especially seniors, with my experience with the mortgage company. On June 7, 2019, I left his office knowing Mr. Howard would contact the lady who left the letter on my door, and I was not ready to address her.

On Monday, June 10, 2019, I was resting in my room. My children ran into my room saying a woman was beating on the door. They were scared. I was upset because she was banging loudly on the door. When I opened the door, she asked, "Did you get my letter?" I said, yeah, "I got your letter." The look on my face told her I did not understand her rationale for coming to my front door. After all, I am the same type of person. However, I knew she could see my children through the glass and see them scared. My face had an I am pissed looked. My tone said, if you hit my door one more time, I might drag you inside and do bad things to you. She scanned my body language.

I told her I had received the letter, and she should expect a call from my lawyer. She asked why I needed a lawyer, and I explained I needed a lawyer to fight the illegal sale of my home. She was stunned that Ihad obtained a lawyer. Over time, the new owner's tone changed. Maybe she recognized I was no longer a deadbeat in her view. I was a woman fighting to keep my home. She was a woman trying to secure the property she had purchased at auction. We were not enemies. She left, and I went back to my room to start planning to move.

I went back to sleep. I needed the rest. Once I got up, I said, "okay, I'm going to get the storage and the boxes. I'm going to move". I proceeded to move while my children were in summer camp. I did that every day. When I picked them up, I explained why we were moving. My children were concerned about leaving their schools. I continued to focus on keeping my family feeling like things would be okay. I didn't want them to see me break down and cry all the time. I didn't feel like crying while I waspacking and moving.

Chapter 7

Time to Move

The first thing I needed was to rent a storage unit. I had never rented a storage unit in my life. I did not believe in using storage units because people store items they do not need for years. People pay on them for life. I found storage unit around the corner from my home in Pearland. I did not get the size right, so I got a second unit. I was able touse their truck for free too. I move most of my items in the back of my Nissan Rogue. I learned you could let the seats down and move an entire house in a Nissan Rogue. I moved all my pictures and my kitchen items. I moved my stuff by myself every day from June 10, 2019, until I moved outof the house on June 26, 2019.

I paid my landscaper to help me move all the heavy stuff. My children helped me pack items in the truck and car, and I moved while they were in early in the morning. God gave me a perfect time to move because my children were out of school. I lost weight moving. It was hot in the storage unit. I learned to get rid of items I did not need or want. I kept the storage units for one month. When you must move quickly, material objects hold less weight than you initially think. My children asked tons of questions during the process. I could not answer many of their questions, but I kept myself together. I was honest with them.

I did not tell my oldest son what was happening. I didn't tell anybody that I was moving. The people who knew I was moving did not volunteer to help me. I learned having an unrealistic expectation of others caused problems. I re-evaluated the people in my life during this time. I knew some of the people in my life were good to have a conversation with,but they were not in my life to help me do the heavy lifting.

No Evictions

I learned some buyers are willing to pay owners to move out without damaging their homes. I found it strange people would damage their own home. I spent almost six months picking out items for my house and praying for the sale to go through; why would I want to destroy it. My sister reminded me that everyone who has their house stolen via foreclosure did not move out quietly. In their anger, they did damage to their home, and sometimes they sold items from home. To prevent this type of behavior, buyers offered homeowners a check for the keys to their homes.

My lawyer said he could get me some money in exchange for me moving without damaging my home. However, he wanted to make sure I was ready to walk away from my plan to keep my home. While talking with Mr. Howard, I became willing to move on with my life. He agreed to speak with the buyers. To rebound from homelessness, it helps to have an attorney. I hated that I did not get a lawyer initially, but I was glad I secured one when I did. I needed him to handle the things I could not address. I needed him for where I was in the process.

Hiring Mr. Howard provided me with some of my dignity. When I left the district, I lost some of my resilience, and I was too physically and mentally beat down to fight this last battle by myself. I hired him to protectme and my interest. It felt good to hear someone ask me, "What do you want, Dr. Pope? What do you need to move forward?" He gave me back my sense of control in the situation I felt had zero control. I knew I wanted and needed a check, and I knew I needed money to move.

When my sister said everyone who goes through foreclosure gets evicted, I became adamant that it would not happen. I could not accept an eviction on my credit. I did not understand why an eviction triggered my fears so much. I didn't want to be an evicted 50-year-old, African American female entrepreneur with a doctorate in psychology. When my sister told me getting evicted was part of the process, I became defiant. I became more determined I would not be evicted. I told her I would leaveon my own accord, but I would not because of an eviction.

My sister explained how the eviction process would happen. Her father was a realtor, and she learned how the process worked. She explained how the Sheriff's Department was responsible for evicting homeowners. She explained they would put a colored piece of paper on my door, the Scarlett red letter for evicted homeowners. She said the documents would be fluorescent. Fear immediately consumed me when she talked about the Sheriff's Department. I was an active Silver Level member of the Pearland Chamber of Commerce, and our Sheriff was a member. Most of the local business owners were members of the Pearland Chamber of Commerce. I was also a member of the Brazoria County HispanicChamber of Commerce.

I joined both rooms to help me grow my business. I knew joining the chambers would allow me to connect with women like myself. I never once thought I would lose my home, and I was shaking with the thought that everyone would know and judge me. While sharing my fears with my sister, she reminded me that I needed to accept that people in my community would know my secret. I mentally pictured the neighbors across the street to seeing my downfall. I imagined my neighbors on both sides of my house driving by and seeing the scarlet letter on my door. Ifmy neighbors wanted to know when I sold my home, they could go to the County Clerks' office. A fluorescent sign from the Sherriff's Department door said I was evicted.

The day came when a lady from the Sheriff's Department came to serve me a court date. That lady was so kind to me. She smiled and handled me with care. The first thing I said to her was, "You didn't put the note on the door. I told her my fear of having a big letter F on D on my door." She gave me the neon green sign in my hand. She gave me so much respect and allowed me to keep my dignity. She smiled, and I smiled. She hugged me. I needed that hug more than she knew. I couldn't have asked for a better person to deliver the paperwork. She did her job, but she treated me with respect.

Although I received the letter to appear in court in front of the local Justice of the Peace, who was a member of the Pearland Chamber of Commerce, too, I still had an option to avoid being evicted. Mr. Howard reminded me I had a few cards to play regarding the outcome of this nightmare, and I decided I wanted to move by the end of the month. When he talked to the new owners, they agreed to give me until June 26, 2019, to leave my home. They also decided not to file eviction and gave me a check for $1000.00 to leave the home in its beautiful condition. I decided to give them the keys and not harm their new investment. They bought my house as an investment property.

After I got the call from Mr. Howard telling me the good news, I proceeded to pack up my stuff to move. I had a little more energy because I did not get evicted. I knew I had favor from God during the process. I talked with my children about our abrupt move. I was frank with them. They saw me moving our stuff for the rest of the month. They witness my first time driving a short rental truck. I accidentally backed it into my garage. The truck was fine. The garage had a little dent. When I hit it, it popped back into place. I did not know how to back it up. It's funny, but I did not see how I would move forward in my life. Nor could I see how to go backward correctly in the truck. My vision for my life was literally and figurately shot. I could not see where I was going in any direction. I wore glasses, but I realized my peripheral vision was horrible. I was so happy my sister told me to get a storage unit with access to a free moving truck. I did not know movers had so many options. When I moved before, I paid for professional movers. This time I did the work. I selected a storage unit close to my house to avoid mileage fees. God had things lined up for me to move forward in my life slowly. I learned to drive the truck.

I decided I was not taking my love seat and sofa. They were not in good condition when I moved out. They were too big to move in my Nissan. They were the last items I needed to move on my last day in the house. I heard the trash truck coming down the street, so I decided to ask the sanitation engineers to help me move the sofa and love seat out of my home. I walked outside and flagged them down. They agreed to help me, and I paid them $20.00 in cash. They put the sofa and love seat on the sidewalk. I realized I had to ask for help early during the moving process.

Everything I wanted to take to my new home was in two storage units. A few items did not make it to the storage that I wanted. When the new owner came to get the keys, I had not been able to get everything in storage. I put my bedroom pillows, my containers filled with rice, flour, and sugar, my trash cans, and my two housewarming gifts from my mother. The plaque she gave me was priceless to me. I had the following quote, "For I know the plans I have for you," declares the Lord, "Plans to prosper you, plans to give you hope, and a future" (Jeremiah 29:11). See Figure I needed to see and read the quote. I had to believe God had a better plan for me that I could not see at that moment. I also left my grill on the back patio. I wanted to take my lemon tree, but it was too big. For the first time in four years, it was full of lemons. I wanted to see the lemons change colors and eat at least one of them. I prayed so much for that lemon tree over the years. I left those items in haste to move and not break myagreement with the new owners.

We had a few things my children wanted to keep with them in the car. I did not want to have too much with us on the road. When people saw stuff in the car, I did not want to motivate them to steal it. After I moved, my initial plan was to call my father and drive to his place in Shreveport, Louisiana. After moving the rest of my stuff to the storage units, I quickly realized that I needed a place to sit for a minute to regroup mentally. I was tired. When I walked out of my home for the last time, it hurt more than I anticipated. I was ready to move, but the pain was extreme. I didn't have anapartment rented to quickly move into with my children and my dog, Danny. I needed to regroup. I needed to figure out how to proceed with three children and a dog in a dirty Nissan Rogue.

I used a third-party rental to reserve a room at a local hotel chain in Pearland. I made a mistake with the reservation. I should've called the hotel directly. I had to cancel the reservation, and the third-party business tried to keep my room costs. I sat in the hotel's parking lot, and I cried and screamed in the car. I had a moment! My children quickly stopped talking. For a moment, I released my pain and anger about having to leave my home of six years because I decided to accept a plan that led to the theft of my house. I did not have the energy for one more fight. I quickly found Motel 6 in Webster. After I checked into my room, we ate at the Waffle House located in the same parking lot as the motel. Once again, God provided while I tried to take more steps forward.

Chapter 8

New Adventure

The next day, I realized I had left my items outside on the couch. I decided to drive by and see if they were still there. Some of the things were there. Someone took my pillows and trash cans, but they left the flour, rice, sugar, and my two housewarming gifts. I left the food. I did not want to jump the fence to get the grill and a few lemons. The last thing I wanted my neighbors to see was me jumping the fence. I took my two housewarming gifts and drove to my dad's house in Louisiana.

When we arrived in Shreveport, everything seemed fine. My dad received a subsidy for his living arrangements. Therefore, there were rules about guests. My dad failed to tell me about the rules and how they would impact my stay. I discovered he could only have guests for a short time. Dogs were not allowed. I was disparately looking for an apartment. I bought food because I knew we were eating more than he planned to provide. I arrived on Saturday, and I planned to drive to Houston on Monday to secure a place to stay. I could leave my children and the dog with my dad while I went back to Pearland. My children did not want to stay with my dad. I ended up driving with them from Shreveport, La to Pearland.

Housing in Pearland

I visited a nice apartment complex before I moved from Pearland. My former realtor told me about the apartment complex, so I decided to apply. I completed the application on-site. It was a long and tedious process. They wanted to know everything except for my shoe size and weave color. I am using hyperbole, but they asked a vast number of questions. I had not lived in an apartment for six years and was unaware things had changed so much. I didn't understand their process. I called my sister and told her about my experience. She said the apartment complex was a housing complex. I told her Pearland did not have any housing. I noticed I saw more African Americans coming in and out of the office. I lived in Pearland for over 15 years, and I never saw too many African Americans concentrated in one location. I also lived in a subdivision with a few African Americans. I learned a lot through this whole process. If I had known about the complex, I would have campaigned there when running for City Council. I found out the complex could not vote in Pearland City elections.

The application had so many questions. It was ridiculous, but I filled it out. The lady that helped me declared, "this isn't enough information." My sister told me I was applying for low-income group (LIG) housing. The woman who helped me became obsessed with finding out how much money I received from the sale of my home. I told her repeatedly I never received any money from the sale of my house. The apartment manager did understand no one gave me any documents regarding the sale of my home.

Another lady was working in the office. She asked me again how much income I receive from the sale of my home. Again, I told her I never received any money. She argued with me and said, you must have received some money. My house was not sold by its owner. I had not been through the process before, so I did not respond to her questions. I was also irritated because they asked me all the questions in front of whoever was in the office. The manager finally got involved and yelled out her questions from her office in the back. I had lost my dignity, but I was not going to lose my mind in the office at the complex. They were loud and acted like I was lucky they were taking the time to help me complete the application. They had never heard of the word discretion.

Finally, I admitted my house was sold at auction. I told her I did not receive any money. Admittedly, I did not have any paperwork to give her. The office worker insisted I explain how I failed to generate income from the sale of my home. I said, "Madam, I didn't get any money from my house sale; I should have received money from the sale of my home. Instead, I did not receive any proceeds from the sale. There was a $33,000 difference between what I owed on the house and the purchase price. I only found out I was supposed to get the difference from selling my home at auction because one of my former students, Octavia, called me and explained the law and the process. I went to the Brazoria County Courthouse and found the paperwork showing the sale of my home. My Brazoria County Appraisal District (BCAD) appraised my home's value of $228,000. It sold for $192,000.00 at auction. I purchased my home for $166,610.00, and I owed a balance of $159 000.00. I told her I contacted the title company that handled the sale of my house. They said to me since I had a lawyer, they could not talk with me. While I explained what happened to me, I became overwhelmed by shame and anger. I drove back to Shreveport to wait for the approval.

When I arrived at my dad's place, he explained he would have an inspection, and I did not think much of it. I told him I was going back to Pearland to speak with the manager again. I went back on Wednesday because I did not hear anything regarding approval. The management requested more information. I was tired, but I pushed on back to Shreveport, Louisiana.

I figured out I had to decide where I wanted to stay for at least a year. I needed to look at more than the price of an apartment. I felt like I was regressing while I looked for an apartment. I had to push past my thoughts while I searched for a location. I didn't particularly appreciate how I was treated during the process. I had to listen to my spirit too. I drove back to Shreveport the same night. When we walked into my dad's home, he told me that we could not stay in his apartment anymore. I looked at him in disbelief. I asked him if he wanted me to give his manager proof of my situation. I asked him to give me a week to find something. He said the manager told him he violated his lease. I was hurt, but I did not say anything else. The next day was July 3rd. I called my uncle to see if we could stay with him, but I quickly realized it was not an option. I called my mother, and she said I could live with her in Elgin, TX.

I packed up my items, my children, and my dog. I left the food I purchased for him. My father did not come out of his room until he was sure I had packed everything and was leaving. I told my children to say goodbye to their grandfather. I knew our relationship was never going to be the same moving forward. I felt a pain that was sharp but not lethal. Again, this experience taught me to accept my reality. Having faith in God does not mean you should have faith in people doing the right thing. I did not speak to my dad for five to six months after that day. I had to try to understand his rationale for putting us out while I was desperate for a place to stay. My dad had put himself first in all his relationships with women. I thought because I was his daughter, he would handle me differently. However, I learned his need for self-preservation was more important than my salvation. Once I accepted that he was unwilling to lose his apartment, I understood and accepted his decision. I realized I was putting his place in jeopardy. I did not want everyone to be homeless. I decided that day that I never make any decisions regarding my father that would cause me any guilt or discomfort. The relationship was different between myself and my father. Although I forgave my dad and loved him, I handled him differently.

Chapter 9

Another Move

I moved to my mother's guest house when I left my dad. I was tired. My sister and my mom arranged things in the guest house to stay there in peace. I know someone thinks I did not have it rough. Some may be saying I lived in a guest house and was not on the street or in a shelter; therefore, I was not homeless. When I went to the public library in Elgin, TX, and the lady asked me for my ID, I realized I was homeless. I loved taking my children to the library. For the first time, my children could not check out books. I could have asked my mother to use her library card, but I was too outdone when I realized I was homeless. When I moved, I did not have a place to forward my electricity, water, or cable because I was homeless. I forgot to deliver my mail to my PO Box, so I failed to get vital information regarding my bank accounts. I did not have a key to unlock or lock the guest house because I was homeless.

My kids were safe. My mom lived in a beautiful subdivision. She lived next door, so she did not hear us in her guest house. It was peaceful, and I needed a safe space. While we lived there, my mom made us feel welcomed. I needed rest, time to regroup and get myself together. My mom was not planning to let us stay for an extended period, and I could not have a pity party. She did not explicitly say I need you gone by a specific date. Although my mother had a washer and dryer, I had to take our clothes to the laundromat. My children learned about the utility of a roll of quarters, and they also learned how to wash, dry, and fold clothes quickly.

I found solace on her couch. I laid on it for hours because living in Elgin was not my plan, and I needed to hear from God on my next move. I knew the moment I laid on the couch that I was not driving anywhere for a few days. I wasn't ready to get up and drive back and forth to Pearland. Thenext day my mom asked me what's was going on with the apartment. I told her I was waiting to find out. It was Independence Day, but we did not celebrate. We spent the entire day moving stuff around my mom's guest house. My mom was getting frustrated because I was touching her stuff. My mom's guest house had cable; it was clean and beautiful. We had a bathroom. We had a kitchen without a stove, but we had a refrigerator. Thebedroom was upstairs, but we slept downstairs.

I was so grateful that we had a place to live, and it was summer. My children were out of school, and if there was an excellent time for me to be homeless, the summer was it. I was free to move two additional times without disrupting my children's schoolwork. Luckily, I worked for myself too, and I did not have to explain or worry about absences or childcare. I was able to take things in and accept what happened. I sat on the couch andreleased my fears.

My children played outside. My mom would – ask what we were going to eat. She brought us food to eat. I was so grateful that I did not have to pay her right away. My mom never mentioned money, but I knew I would have to pay if I lived somewhere else for 22 days. I paid for our food, and sometimes she brought us take-out meals. She helped us tremendously. Although my mother helped us, she did things that bothered us too. While I lived in my mom's guesthouse, I knew I had to follow her rules. My mom conducted a walk-through inspection. I could tell she had been looking around. She blamed my children for clogging the toilet in the guest house. I would explain the bathroom was like that when we arrived. She would also tell us to turn the air off when we left.

She did not care if the air was running during the day, but she wanted it to be off if we were not using it. I did not blame her for watching her bills. My mom's walk through visits was a reminder that her guest house was not my place. We were guests. I had to adjust to her rules and expectations.

Suddenly I was dealing with shame again. I wouldn't say I liked that I was a grown woman who lived in her mother's guest house, and I felt the need to defend my children. My mom had a bunch of toys in the guesthouse that she did not want the children to touch. My children got into her rubber bands and designed some necklaces, and I did not think anything of it because it kept them busy. She was upset; then, I was upset because I had to keep reminding my children to respect her property and to leave her stuff alone.

While I was lying on the couch, I was constantly thinking. We had become close because we had been together every day since June 26, 2019. I was trying to move quickly, and I had to ask people for money and help get money to move. I also decided I did not want to live in housing. Although I wanted to move quickly, I realized that the apartment complex was not for me. First, I did not want to live in public housing. One of my concerns was the cap on my income potential. If I went over the income requirement levels, I had to move. My goal was not to stay poor. More importantly, I could not stand dealing with the disrespect I received during the application process. I did not make much money, but I knew my finances would change. The invasion of my privacy was too much for me to endure during the application process. I could not see myself living there for a year. I was still waiting on them to tell me if I was approved. I decided to call and let them know I would not move forward with the process. I learned I was trying to move forward quickly, but I also had to maintain my standards. I realized some doors were closed for a good reason. The apartment complex was the wrong place. God had a protective hedge around me, and I did not need to remove it.

I realized I had not attended my church on Wednesdays anymore. I decided to drive to Houston to attend Lakewood again. Pastor John Gray was a fire on Wednesday nights! While going to church, I would ask God for His help. I praised Him too. The song "Oceans" by Hillsong UNITED became my anthem. I never lost my faith during the process. However, I felt my mental and physical battle with the school district and the mortgage company had pushed me to where I did not trust my judgment. I knew I could rely on God. I knew if I relied on my strength, I would not move forward. I understood I had to trust Him to keep me above the waves:

You call me out upon the waters

The great unknown

Where feet may fail

And their I find You in mystery

In oceans deep

My faith will stand

And I will call upon Your name

And keep my eyes above the waves

When the oceans rise

My soul will reset in Your embrace

For I am Yours

You are mine

My relationship with God grew stronger because He was providing. I didn't understand all my journey. I didn't know why I had to lose my home. I did not understand the disrespect I encountered along the way. I was not too fond of some of the things I learned about my inner circle. My air conditioner died on one of my trips back from Houston. It was hot, but I did not have enough money to repair the air. My car needed more than freon to fix the problem. It took me a year to get AC in my vehicle.

When I started examining which direction I would go, I was a certified teacher. I can teach anywhere in the state of Texas. So, I can always visit the school district's HR department. Whenever I need to earn money to take care of my family, I know I can return to teaching. As I looked at the walls in Elgin's central office, I was able to see the district's student population was mainly Caucasian. I did not see any African American teachers on the wall. I had to consider those facts.

While living in my mom's guest house, I could work in Elgin and get myself together. I thought about staying with her for a year while paying rent, and I would be able to keep my family in a stable environment. Unfortunately, my children insisted we return to Pearland. I tried to figure out what I needed to do to keep my production business. I thought I could drive to Houston to film my show and projects. I could teach full-time too. I realized instantly I was unrealistic. I wasn't going to work all day again as a teacher. And I was thinking, too, if I didn't want to do teaching, what else could I do for a regular check? There's a college there. Austin community college was not that far from my mom's house. I said, well, I could apply to work as an adjunct professor. I love that I have a craft that I can take anywhere and work. I was qualified to be an administrator and a school counselor. I could be anything. I could even be a substitute teacher. I was willing to do anything to start bringing in some income.

And then I was nervous because I had to say, how are you going to like, meet your needs with your business? I told my children we might stay in Elgin. I remember one day my mom came in the guest house and reminded me that I left the air conditioner on while we were out. That was the day I realized I couldn't stay permanently. It was her house, but I didn't want her coming into the guest house telling me I left the air or giving me a reminder.

I drove back to Pearland on July 26, 2019. I found my new residence in Pearland. Once I completed the application, I was approved instantly. I was able to secure the apartment by paying the deposit. My income from my small business was enough to get me approved for my apartment and my automobile, and I did not need to live in housing.

Chapter 10

Asking for Help

One of the hardest things I had to do while rebounding from homelessness was to ask for help. If I had asked for help earlier, I might have avoided the entire mess. I did not know who I could trust with my secret. I hated hearing the word no. I hated rejection. I did not know who had the money and would be willing to extend me grace. Another issue I had was taking too much pride in being the helper or servant in my inner circle. When the people around you can never help you, you need to change the people around you. I hated to admit most of the people around me wanted me to help them. They called me for help. Being homeless pushed me to a point where I had to surrender; I had a limited number of real friends.

More importantly, I accepted I was not the same after two stressful battles back-to-back. I lost my will to fight needless battles. I learned to acknowledge my weakness. I recognized at my age; I did not have time for foolishness. I lost my willingness to take on too many challenges at one time. I had to identify and eliminate people who were time wasters and takers. I had to stop working with people who had dreams but were unwilling to make them come to manifestation. I to tell people my life was not perfect. I did not want to hear people tell me what they would do if it were them. I did not want to listen to people tell me to get a job. I hated arguing with people who were scared to leave their jobs but wanted to complain about them all day. I did not want to hear everyone's judgment ofme and my decisions.

I also had to acknowledge my issues with money had come to a point where I could not allow it to continue to control me anymore. I hated being poor growing up. People have low expectations of poor people. I spent most of my adult life running from poverty. I worked hard to achieve and acquire things that indicated I was not lacking, like my house. I loved being a single African American female homeowner. I worked hard to achieve the American dream.

I was proud to become a full-time entrepreneur when I started my business. When I started my business full-time, I had no idea how poor I would become again. I had no idea how much owning a business required me to commit to walking by faith. I did not see how important it was for me to change my mindset about poverty and shame. I used to hate when my mom paid for our groceries with food stamps before she became a registered nurse. I refused to accept assistant from the welfare system. The battle with shame and money finally came to a head during this process.

The other problem with asking for help is trusting others to respect your privacy and vulnerability. I did not know how to share clients werenot paying me, and I felt it made me look weak. Sometimes, you tell others your problems and use them against you. I created my organization, Boss Ladies Professional Network because I realized I was lonely trying to be a Boss. I took a risk that people with jobs did not understand. I needed to find out what other women were doing to succeed in business.

The first person I reached out to for help was my friend named Dana. Dana called after I moved to my mom's guest house. I took the call because I thought it might be an opportunity to ask her to loan me money for a deposit for my electric services. She called because she had listed me as a reference for a job, and she was checking on the referral status. I interrupted her concerns about using me for a connection to let her know about my concerns. I made my ask, and she told me she would call me back. Instead of calling me back, she texted me her answer. She told me, "Ineed to get a job." She also gave me a link to a Higher-Ed to search for ajob.

Our friendship was fragile before the call; it was dead after her text. Our friendship did not end because she did not give me the money. It ended because of the way she handled my situation and my feelings. Months later, she wrote me and explained her situation. She maintained shedid not think because she had her crisis. I believed her. I was not ready to move forward with our friendship at that moment. Nevertheless, I didforgive her a couple of months later.

I forgave her because I had known her for years, and she had neverdone anything to harm me. She had been good to my children and me before this moment. She gave me gifts for Christmas and birthdays, and we had issues before this tragedy. Sometimes it is better to judge a person by their history with you than just a moment. Honestly, my emergency was not her emergency. Her words hurt, but she told me what she felt was the solution to my problem. She told me what other people were thinking but were scared to say. My friends and family felt if I had a job, I would not bein my situation. They failed to accept my business was my full-time job!

I ended my friendship with Dana due to the cowardly way that she responded to my request. I would have understood if she told me she did not have the money. She had done other things for me in the past. I was hurt because I had to be so vulnerable to share my story with her. Her response was harsh and cold.

I had never asked her for anything in our 10-year friendship. Immediately when I read the text repeatedly, I thought about all the time she called and expected me to provide my business services free of charge for her students. I thought about several things when I read the text repeatedly, and I laughed out of disbelief a couple of times.

At that moment in my life, I did not need a text telling me to get a job. I knew how to look for one. I needed money for a deposit for electricity. Getting a job required time, and I needed money quickly. Her solution was a slap in my face. The most hurtful part was her expectation of me to continue to be a reference, and I knew she should never list me as a reference again. After a few months passed, she took the time to apologize for how she handled me. I accepted the apology. We do not speak regularly, but I have zero anger or bitterness over the incident.

Although my mother helped me by providing shelter during my storm, she did not give me any money to help me move forward with securing an apartment. She had money, but she was not offering it to me. She told me to ask my friends for help, and I could not respond to her without saying something that would have set her off. I knew better than to bite the hand that fed me. I knew who I needed to call, but I did not want to make the call. I could have called her when I needed my mortgage payment. She had helped me before with my car.

Instead of moving on to the next person on my "People Who MightHelp Me List," I was focused on what my mother was not doing to helpme. God reminded me of something I had learned earlier. I knew people would help others in the manner they saw fit. People rarely ask the person in need what type of help they want. The person who needs to be rescued cannot control or demand specifics from their "rescuers." There is an underlining assumption when helping others. People in need must be grateful when rescuers provide any help. For example, if the person needs to pay their electric bill, they need cash, not a gift card to Target. If the person in need rejected the gift card and asked for money to pay the electric bill, the "rescuer" might become offended. Instead of seeing the person in condition with empathy, they will see them as ungrateful or extra. The "rescuer" has the power in the relationship. People who help others have different motives, and they will let the person in need know when you have stepped over the imaginary boundaries in the relationship.

My mother helped me the best way she felt she could. I wanted herto do more, but she had done what she felt was best for herself and me.

Dani helped the way she felt was best for herself. My need for $300.00 was not Dani's responsibility, and she did not try to make it her responsibility. I gave and helped so many people because I took on their responsibilities. I became too involved. I do not do that anymore. I support based on what works for my life, schedule, and resources since 2019.

Once I understood the assignment, I stepped out of my mom's guest house, dialed Kodi's number, and began to walk around in circles on the leaves in my mother's yard. I could hear them crack underneath my feet as I kept pacing. I was terrified to address her. I was ashamed because I had not told her what was happening because I did not want or need her judgment. I had to call her at this point because my options were limited. Since moving out of my home, I started to cry for the first time. The tears ran down my face quickly because I was ashamed. I began to cry because I had spent every dollar to pay the deposit and the rest of the rent for July, and I still needed to pay the first month's rent and get the lights turned on before moving into the apartment.

When Kodi answered, I could barely speak. I am never at a loss for words. I cried the entire time during the call. I cried because I was humiliated and embarrassed that she had been so kind to help me before I had trouble with the house. She had been the friend who helped me move past my divorce. She had been there to help me pack my office when my lease ended. She was always there to help my children and me. She was my professional mentor. I had so much respect for her. I did not call her to tell her about the community leaders who did not pay me because she told me to stop working with them earlier. She felt like most of the people I worked with always tried to take advantage of my kindness. I could not tell her she was right, and I paid too high of a price this time. I did not ask her for money when I was short on my mortgage payment. I knew if I borrowed money then, I would need it again. I could not call her one more time for help.

It hurt to explain that I turned off the lights when I moved because I couldn't transfer my services anywhere. I did not cry before this moment. A few tears hit the pillow I was holding over my face while I was screaming, but I had not had a real hard cry. After I stopped screaming, I realized I had to get up and do something. I did not allow myself an opportunity to grieve over the loss of my home, and I did not take the time to sit on my patio and cry. I kept moving from my home to my dad's place to my mother's guest house in a week. When I arrived at my mom's, I started looking for another place to live.

During our conversation, I decided to sit in my car. I did not want my children to walk upon my crying. I have never allowed my children to see my anguish over losing my home. I tried to keep a good attitude. Some days I was not successful. As I sat in my Nissan that Kodi had helped me with the down payment, I thought about my efforts to get me out of my turmoil. My cry was more complex, and I started to process why I cried so much. I cried because I was ashamed and angry. I cried because I felt like my mother, sister, and dad had not helped me in the way I needed their help. However, they helped me!

My dad allowed me to stay long enough to apply for an apartment. When he asked us to leave, he helped me see where I stood in our relationship. I needed to know so I could be free of false expectations. My sister gave me strategies to secure a rental unit and a free truck. She gave me a strong dose of reality! I needed it. She told me about the Money for Key Program, and she helped prepare the guest house for me, my children, and my dog. My mother allowed me to stay for as long as I needed toobtain a new apartment. She allowed me to invade her privacy and to access her things. I had help, but my expectations differed from what I expected to happen. My expectations of others have been a significant issue for me professionally and personally.

I cried because some of the people I expected to do something did nothing. I was disappointed and angry when people learned what was happening but failed to help. Some people did not know what was happening, so they could not help. While I was expecting certain people to help, I later realized that God had people to help me. They were in the rightplace at the right time to help me. Former students helped so much.

They shared their knowledge, their time, and their resources. The Sanitation Engineers (trashmen) came down the street to move the sofa and love seat. My neighbor kept my children on the last day while I put the last few itemsowned in storage.

To rebound, I had to learn how to receive help from people who God touched to help me. I had to know many of those God sent to help did not wear the label friend or family member. More importantly, I learned many of the people I had helped over the years in the community did not help me. Again, I learned because I helped people did not mean those same people would aid me in my time of need. I know how to help people without any expectations of reciprocity, and I will never be disappointed.

Kodi agreed to give me the money to help me secure my apartment. I was happy about that, but I still felt some shame. She had provided me with her requirement for paying back the money, and I agreedto everything she required. I was excited had found a place, and I was ready to move forward to our new home.

Chapter 11

The New Place

When I looked for the new apartment, I looked for something I could afford. I wanted to stay within my $1300 a month budget. My budget was realistic. I wanted three bedrooms with two baths. It did not have everything I wanted when I found the first one. My second option was in the same apartment complex. It was a brand-new upstairs unit with stainless steel appliances. I knew my children would give my downstairs neighbors the blues with all the running and walking they would do daily. The third apartment seemed familiar. Immediately, I knew it was my place because there was a granite countertop almost the same color and pattern I had in my previous kitchen. The dark brown cabinets matched my chairs and everything else I had. I thanked God for the confirmation. The new apartment was my landing place, and it matched my taste. The floors were concrete, but they had a hardwood floor design. I loved the place. I also knew I wouldn't say I liked the idea of breathing hard while I crawled up and down stairs daily.

I asked the apartment manager if they had another apartment with the same look but downstairs. When I was trying to rebuild my life, I realized the importance of not settling for anything that I could not commit to paying for again. If I were going to commit to living in a place,

I would be there until I could get approved for another house. My plan in July 2019was to stay in the apartment until I improved my credit and saved a nice down payment for my next home and generate more revenue from mysmall businesses.

My children were the driving force behind many of the choices. When I decided to return to Pearland, TX, my children insisted on moving. We moved forward as a team. I'm proud that I included my children in most of the decisions during that year. Growing up, I did not have a say in any decisions, and I did not want my children to feel lost while moving us forward.

The most important thing that happened while securing my apartment was using my income from my business to secure my apartment.It was a massive deal for me. When I purchased my home, the loan was approved based on my employment at Houston Independent School District and Texas Southern University. In 2013, my company did not generate enough income to support my financial needs. However, once I started working full-time for myself in 2017, I could make enough money to pay all my bills and pay myself a small salary. I was able to finance my car based on the profits from my business.

I secured a two-bedroom and a two-bathroom apartment. I'm happy with it, except it did not have a room for my baby boy to have his space. I decided to buy a sleeper sofa. When I was ten years old, I slept on a sleeper sofa in the living room just like J.J. and Michael in *Good Times.*

I got to get rid of my love seat and sofa from my home. They were deplorable anyway. I planned to purchase new furniture, but I did not want any debt. I decided to use my patio furniture in the living room. When I slept on my patio sofa, I felt great. I was ashamed of having the patio furniture in the living room, but the option of sitting on the floor did not work for me.

Then I got in my room, and I thought, okay, this is it, and really and honestly, that's all I had when I moved in. I moved in with a ton of stuff from the house. However, I gave away my refrigerator, entertainment center, lawnmower, and other items because I refused to pay for storage beyond one month. I'm still giving away or throwing things away. It isn't easy me to move my four-bedroom home into my two-bedroom apartment.

When we found the apartment, I knew I had to make some adjustments. My baby boy would not have his room for a while, and I needed to purchase a let-out couch so he could sleep in the living room. I slept on a let-out couch when I was ten, and I enjoyed it on the show "Good Times" Michael and J. J. slept on one too. There were going to be some downsides to it, but we had to make it work until I could do better.

I planned to work as a substitute teacher in several school districts and apply as an adjunct at HCC, and I would have a flexible schedule and still run my business. I received a text from the Executive Assistant of the English Department of Texas Southern University. They needed an adjunct right away. I went right over there to secure a position because I needed the money. God had once again touched people to help me.

Chapter 12

The Unexpected

I started working at TSU on August 15th, but I did not get paid because we did not begin work officially, according to the paperwork, until September. So, after I paid her Kodi back the money I borrowed for the rent, I was busted. I was happy to pay her as promised because I did not want any issues. I started worrying about the next month's rent. I needed to pay her back the money she loaned me to secure the deposit for my electricity. I agreed to pay her $100 a month. Somewhere during my payments, I did not pay her on time. I think it was the second payment. She sent me an email telling me she needed her money. I was so shocked at the tone. To be honest, I was shocked she said she needed her money because I knew $100 was not going to hurt her life. I became defensive, and I was hurt. I asked myself whether she heard me crying. I questioned if she thought after I had paid her back the big loan as promised that I would try not to pay the $100. I thought the email was unnecessary. Her email was a very pronounced way to say make your payment, and I understood her point. I will never agree that she needed to send me an email. I felt we were close enough for her to call, check on me, and see if I realized I had not paid. She was the second person in my circle to use a text to deliver a crappy message.

I was in my feelings, and I determined I would not destroy our friendship over money. When I was completing my doctorate, a friend of mine told me, "Sheila, when you have your head in the lion's mouth, you cannot jerk it out! You must wait until the right time and carefully remove it." While I owed her money, my head was in the lion's mouth. Again, shame had crept back into the picture. I never addressed my feelings about the email. I made sure to drop off the money. When Kodi was not home, I would put it in an envelope and slide it under her door. When I had an extra $400, I decided to pay off the balance in one lump sum. I felt so proud of myself. I did not receive any more emails from her.

The day I went to pay my last payment, I felt relieved. My head was out of the lion's mouth. I was not talking to many people because I was scrambling to adjust. I was still embarrassed that I had put myself in the position to ask her for help. The side effects from the abrupt move had me scared to unpack my stuff. I was in the apartment for a year before unpacking all the boxes. I was always waiting for a shoe to drop.

When I arrived, she asked if I wanted to come in and talk. She was insistent. I did not want to speak because I was still processing the need for the email. When I agreed to go in and talk, she asked me what was going on with me. I told her some of what was happening. Again, I was not sharing any information with her or anybody else. I was so beat down. I thought she, of all people, knew my pain. Then, she said her friends asked about her me, and she told them I had a nervous breakdown. I stopped and looked at her. Her statement so caught me off guard. I knew I was profusely crying when I called to ask her for the money, but to tell people I had a nervous breakdown was too much for me to process now. I did not have a nervous breakdown. I was embarrassed when I thought of her friends, believing I had a nervous breakdown. I immediately remembered why I hated being vulnerable and why I hated having to ask others for help. I left that day engulfed in shame and humiliation. I was also glad I had paid her off.

More important, I did not say anything to harm our friendship further. Moving forward, I understood our relationship would be different. I am forever grateful for Kodi's help because I wouldn't have been able to secure an apartment without it. I disagreed with her characterization of my pain, but I knew she gave me money when no one else would. I know she had been there for me through so much, and I could not allow what shesaid to erase her kindness and generosity to my children.

Friendship requires forgiveness. I knew I had to forgive Kodi's words for moving forward. We have started back having lunch and talking on the phone. I could not sit and chat when I was trying to rebuild my life.I did not hear from anyone in our circle because I realized they were Kodi'sfriends and not mine. I needed to learn that too. Until she said they had asked about me, I was not thinking about them. After I left her house, I stopped thinking about them. I could not let go of what she said about me. When she told them I had a nervous breakdown, I felt exposed. I was working so hard to keep my mess my secret. After I took some time to examine my heart, I realized Kodi did what she had done for years withme; she was gossiping. Only this time, my mess was part of the Tea for the day.

Things were going well until I received my check from Texas Southern University. I anticipated a more extensive check than I received. I had paid Kodi back but rent rolled around again. When I saw my review was a grand less than I anticipated, I had to sit down on a bench in the courtyard. I called payroll, explained what happened, and showed me my mistake.

I decided this time to use the resources I knew about in the community. I went over the Pearland Neighborhood Center. No more hiding and refusing to say I needed help. I made an appointment and completed tons of paperwork. I told the complex I was going to get help on the rent. They brought up the nasty word eviction again. I told her I was going to get help. She said she would wait to file. I asked her why they filed eviction notices on residents five days late on the rent. I felt that was excessive.

Meanwhile, I was waiting on the approval for the rental assistance. I called and discovered I could not receive help because I had not lived in my apartment long enough. Once again, I complete paperwork only to find out I do not qualify for a program. My head started hurting, my anxiety levels increased, and I began to demand an explanation once again. I asked the person on the phone why the lady who helped me gather and complete the paperwork did not see I was not in the apartment long enough to receive their services. One of the reasons people hate going to social services or non-profits to get help is the bureaucracy. Social service agencies are designed to help people in need. Sometimes the volunteers are working in agencies are often not trained to catch the loopholes. They are giving their time to help others. The lady helping me followed the steps to obtain what was required to complete the application process. She was not the person who decided to approve the application. The money was there, but dumb rules were in place to help the gatekeepers keep the funds. I know Pearland Neighborhood Center is a great agency. Years prior, they helped me before. Once again, they were not the source to help me at that moment.

I was crying again, but I knew I would get the money one way or another. I knew my TSU check would be a consistent source of income for the semester, and I could use it to get a personal loan. Nikki, my former mentee, called me as I parked the car. She knew about the foreclosure, so I was free to vent, and I was pouring out my frustration. While I cried, I could not hear what she asked me. I was spiraling into the why me God mode. I kept repeating, "Why me God? Why me?"

She asked me how much I needed. I told her I had to pay late fees along with the rent. I was about to start screaming again. Then, I heard her say she would give me the money. She had to tell me twice because I was getting ready to tell God a piece of my mind. Although I did not have to ask for help, I still had to accept the help. She asked me when I would be able to pay her back. I told her on October 7th, 2019. I agreed to pay her in two payments. She paid the rent via the portal. I felt so relieved, grateful, and exhausted. I was tired of the roller coaster. I felt like I was constantly battling or fighting the entire year. I was relieved, but once my mind stopped racing, I started to feel overwhelmed by the pressure of having to pay another friend again.

Although she offered, I was still embarrassed, and I did not want to be broke again. I was telling another friend about my issues, and she suggested I ask Nikki if I could pay her back in three payments. My friend was right, but I did not want to call her and sound like I was already changing the loan terms, and I was afraid to rock the boat. I did not call Nikki, and I decided to pay her and move forward. On October 7th, as soon as I had her first payment, I called her. She asked me to drop it off at her place of employment, and I dropped off the payment in cash. I was not happy because the payment hurt me financially. I hurt, but I kept my word. Maybe my face gave me away because she asked me if making the payment was too much for me at the time. I paid her $700.00 instead of $800.00. I left feeling good about myself.

Over the following weeks, I spent a great deal of time with her on the phone and in person. She was helping me in so many ways. Over time, she was a huge blessing and a friend, but I struggled to get back to normal. My children were in school. I was doing some volunteer work. My campaign was over, and I was still hoping no one knew in the community knew about the foreclosure. I was the definition of the working poor. I noticed I was spending a great deal on the phone encouraging her. I am a counselor, so listening to my friends and giving them advice was very natural. I found I was trying to help her figure out issues at work. I was tired after we talked.I was depleting my energy.

At first, I did not find it a problem because she had helped me, and I needed a friend. However, she started to ask too many questions. I hate when people ask me too many questions. I could not give her answers I didnot have for myself. I could not tell her what I was going to do. I was trying to figure out my journey. I told her that she wanted to know too much about my business one day. She laughed, but I was serious. I was starting to feel that I was sharing too much information in my vulnerable state. I was not trusting myself or her motives. I asked whether she was writing an expose on my situation.

After a few weeks, I followed my gut and started to shut my mouth. I started listening more and watching my time. Once I shut my mouth, I wanted to focus on paying Nikki the last payment I owed. She was still helpful, and we did not have issues. I know to listen to my gut about people and situations that make me uneasy.

I felt like I needed to listen to Nikki's complaints about the people on her job. However, I had my issues I was trying to work through. I was going to work every day in a car without AC. I hated to know my paychecks were spent before I received them. I was constantly worried I was going to lose my apartment. Yet I was trying to encourage her and build her ego. I couldn't give any more energy to her because my energy was depleted, and I could not motivate myself. I learned I needed to stop giving out free therapy sessions, and I could not continue to pour into others when I needed to be refreshed. When we talked, I kept the conversations short. Again, my head was in the lion's mouth. I still owed her money, and I did not owe her my soul.

My November check at Texas Southern University (TSU) did not hit my account. We were paid once a month like clockwork. When my deposit did not hit my account, I went to payroll. They said they deposited the money. At first, I picked up my paychecks from the campus, but I started using direct deposit. I gave them my Chase Bank business routing information.

Unfortunately, while I was moving, I forgot to forward my mail for a short time. Chase had closed my business account because I owed them $200.00. When I lost my home, everything else fell by the wayside. I was not checking my mail, and I was only using my checking account via my debit card. My first direct deposit paycheck from TSU sat in electronic limbo. At that moment, I knew I needed to let Nikki know my situation. I think I left her a phone message telling her about the problem. I wasn't expecting her to say not to pay her, but I was expecting her to understand I had no control over the matter. I expected her to allow me to spend the last payment in December 2019. Instead of us talking on the phone, she sent me an email. I was happy it was not a text this time. She told me she needed her money because she had to pay bills too. I was trying to figure out how to pay her and get my check out of limbo. I responded to heremail, explaining what happened and why it happened.

After running around and calling everyone at Chase and TSU to determine who had my paycheck, I learned Chase was holding my paycheck until I paid them $200.00. I asked the representative at Chase to keep the $200 and deposit the rest of the funds into my account, and he refused. He wanted to keep my check for ten days and then send me a statement with the rest of my money. I spent two hours fighting the representative from Chase Bank. I knew they could not keep my check for debt in my business account, and however, they were adamant. Each time Ithought of a quick and straightforward solution to my problems, the gatekeepers in charge wanted to make things too complicated.

In the end, God intervened. I spoke with another representative, and I made a payment agreement. Chase Bank agreed to re-route my deposit back to TSU. Chase sent the funds back to TSU. I had to wait a couple of days to get my money. When I went to pick up my check from TSU, they said I could not pick up the check. For the first time since June 6th, 2019, I was so angry that I was about to act recklessly in public. The lady in the TSU payroll office could see it in my eyes. She noticed I was pacing back and forth. I knew there was a policeman stationed down the hall, but I was ready to go all in to have some control in my life for the firsttime. The staff in TSU's Payroll office saved my career and life! They worked miracles and cut me a check the same day. I will forever be grateful that the lady who worked in payroll acknowledged my pain and anguish and intervened on my behalf. She knew I would not leave without her office, without my check, or a fight.

I knew when I paid Nikki; my children would not have a Christmas. I was still trying to figure out how to pay everyone and have some money. Monthly I receive my teacher retirement statements from Houston Community College. When I saw how much I had in the account,I found my solution to pay Nikki. I wanted to keep my word. I wanted to protect our friendship. I hated I needed her to help more than the day I agreed to take the money. The pressure I felt was overwhelming. My credittook a hit after I started my business, after I started downsizing, and after I lost my home. I had stopped caring. However, my credit was good enough to purchase two homes and several cars at one point in my life. Keeping my word to her meant everything to me. She gave me money when I needed it. She did not string me along with promises to pay my rent. She kept her word too. Again, I valued her friendship too.

I immediately started the process of withdrawing the money from my retirement account. Once again, I was hopeful. I was finally feeling likeI was crawling out of the abyss. Something told me to check over the deposit information. Once again, I gave the wrong banking information. I think my anxiety played a role in my carelessness with my paperwork. Thistime, I spotted the error quickly, and the retirement fund rep could fix the mistake. As soon as the money hit my account, I sent her the money via Zelle. I sent an email telling her the good news. To my surprise, she rejected the money. She sent me a text that said, "I don't take money via Zelle." She requested I drop off the money at her job. I was so outdone. I was angry, too, because I had to overcome so many barriers to get her the money, only to have her reject the payment. I knew for sure she did not want me to come to her job with the anger I was feeling. I did not plan to have a good Christmas. I thought Nikki was pushing her luck by demanding I bring her money to her job. I felt Zelle was the easiest, cheapest, and fastest way to pay her the money.

I was already ashamed and embarrassed to tell her that my business account was closed. I was frustrated that I had to fight to get my paycheck to spend it all on my debts. I refused to go to her job, but I told her I would wire her the money via Walmart MoneyGram. While I was driving to Walmart, she sent me a message saying she would accept it via Zelle. I learned that day, if someone rejects money sent to them via Zelle, itwill not allow the sender to send it again. I went to Wal-Mart and sent the money via MoneyGram.

I sent her an email thanking her for the loan. I knew she was unaware of the extremes I had to go through to repay her. When Nikki refused the Zelle payment and insisted I come to her place of employment, I called her a few names under my to breath. I had to sit down and laugh again at the people I allowed in my inner circle. She knew my trauma and a great deal of my business. She was the one who first described my pain as trauma. How could she just reject all my effort to preserve our friendship and repay her the money? Once again, I felt hegemony was at play. I was right to send her the payment because nothing good would come from a face-to-face meeting at that point. She needed her money, and I needed my dignity.

Be prepared when you ask people and organizations for help; conditions are attached. When you need assistance, your pride will impede you from receiving the support. Shame and embarrassment are emotions that will pass if you remember you deserve help. Remember your situation is temporary. It is essential to count the cost of asking for help. Being vulnerable does not make you weak. Keep your word if you borrow money from friends and family. Relationships will be tested while you make payments. Be careful who you ask for help. All money is not good money. Payday loans allow you to get money without being judged or rejected, but the price you pay is too excessive. If you need food SNAP or TANF as a business owner, apply for it. If you need to go to local food pantries and charities, go and get help. I have used several places in Pearland to ensure I had enough food to feed my children. I learned which ones treat you with kindness and have the best food. I had to open to receive help from places I never saw myself utilizing. I did not have to do anything illegal or unethical to meet my needs. Because you ask a friend for help does not mean they need to know every detail of your business. Share what is necessary for you to get the service.

I was able to keep my friendship with Kodi because it was based on genuine respect and kindness. I had to get out of my feelings and remember how good Kodi was to my children and me for over ten years. When you need financial help, the people who loan you money have the right to ask to dictate the loan terms. If they are not appropriate to you, reject the loan. The people who lend you money have the right to remind you of your agreement via email or text. They do not have to call. When you live in someone's home, they have the right to set the rules for your stay. It is important to remember people do not have to help you with your emergency. When God touches someone to extend kindness, be grateful, remember when you need help, your family and friends may not be the people who help you. Trust God to identify your sources for provision.

Chapter 13

Lessons Learned

When I decided to write this book, I had no idea how much I would cry, and I did not expect it to take a year to write it. Each time I decided to put it aside, I would hear someone on television talk about writing a book. My friend, Dipal, from Houston Community College, reached out and said she was going to be my accountability partner. I am grateful for her support.

She is completing her doctorate, but she took the time to text me and coach me through the last leg of the writing process. I felt God had convinced me that I needed to finish the book at every turn. Bishop T.D. Jakes poured into me on so many occasions via his television ministry. So many things he said motivated me to share how I could keep my apartment, pay off my loans from friends and banks, restore my credit, and move my business back into an office in May 2021.

FIGURE 6. Dr. Pope at Lakewood Church Photo by Author

Forgiveness is Key

I learned that forgiving was the key to me rebounding from homelessness. My willingness to forgive myself and others for their role in my trauma helped free me. It is important to stress I did not forget what happened to me, but I realized I could not hold on to those feelings. I lost my hair, and my anxiety levels were out of control because I held on to anger and unforgiveness when I left the school district. It took the time to forgive myself.

I kept my faith in God throughout the process, which helped me forgive those that hurt me. I had questions, tantrums, and pain throughout my journey. I knew He was working with me to keep my sanity, and I figured out how to let go. It was imperative to keep God first as I took small steps forward. I took time to reflect on the stronghold that I had to break to create a plan of action to start over.

Once I let go of my pain and anger, I created and focused on building my business. I started my television network called Pope TV. I was always a tech girl, but I did not use my other skills when I was working all the time. When I became a television producer, I realized I

FIGURE 7. POPE TV APP ON ROKU AND AMAZON TV Photo by Author

needed my network to create and distribute my content. I could also use the web to produce and distribute other people's content.

When I was fighting to prove my administrators wrong, I never saw myself as anything other than a teacher. Once I let go and forgive my former bosses, I could envision myself building an empire through my media company, Pope's Resource Center, LLC. My television network streams on ROKU TV and Amazon Fire TV via the POPETV app. If I had stayed stuck in my doubt and resentment, I would not have heard the tiny voice in my head saying, you belong on television. You can teach students and adults on a different level. I took the limits off myself and my abilities once I decided to forgive myself and others who tried the end my teaching career. I am so grateful for the push they gave me with my evaluation.

To set goals, I realized I needed to feed my mind as well as my body. To enhance my spirit and nurture my faith, I listened Bishop TD Jakes, John Gray, Joel Osteen, Michael Todd, Steven Furtick, Lisa Harper, Priscilla Shirer Sarah Jakes Roberts, and Dr. Darius Daniels. I attend church at Lakewood. I watch TBN, Hillsong, and other gospel television shows.

To keep my vision and entrepreneurial spirit alive I watch videos and read articles written by founders like Sara Blakely, Tyler Perry, Scooter Braun, Oprah, Tabitha Brown, Guy Raz's —How I Built This, Forbes Women. I read the Wall Street Journal daily. This is a few of sources I use to keep mindset focused on my goals.

Keep the Family's Need First

The next thing I learned on my way to rebound from homelessness was to keep my family at the center of my plans. By restoring my relationship with my oldest son, God showed me it was vital to have compassion for others who are overwhelmed and homeless. My son needed to return home in November 2019. I forgave him and welcomed him home because I could see and hear his frustration while he struggled to keep a roof over his head in Mississippi. I understood his feelings without the need for him to explain them. For the first time in years, I was scared I would not be able to keep a roof over my head. I also learned why many other cultures allow their children to live at home past 18. Pastor Michael Todd said African Americans are the only group who throw their children out at the age of 18 when they are not mature enough to make it. I agree so much with his statement.

Through my process to rebound, I learned my son needed me. I had to learn how to show him support in the way he needed. I had to stop my old parenting behaviors. He is thriving now. I realized families needed to stay together to support each other until the members were mentally ready and financially stable enough to move. My son and I work as a team to help each other accomplish our goals.

I learned I needed to parent my children differently to rebound successfully. I lived in tight spaces with my three children and my dog, Danny, for almost three months, 24-7. My family grew closer, and I learned my children needed me to be home more than I needed to work for someone else's company full-time. I learned to create new traditions for my family. I learned to tell them I love them more. I learned to listen to what they wanted and factor their needs into my decision about where we lived. I would not have moved back to Pearland if they had not been so adamant about moving back.

I Learned to Combat Shame

I had to overcome shame, humiliation, and embarrassment constantly. I had to continually remind myself I was intelligent and capable of making sound business decisions. I read articles or listened to videos about people who overcame barriers to succeed. I listened to the expert on dealing with shame, Brene' Brown.

Work to Restore Your Credit

I had to tackle debts that had fallen into collections and accounts that were closed. I took some time to tackle my credit issues. I am still rebuilding my credit, but I have made tremendous gains. I paid my bills before I lost my home. After the battle with the district, I was not thinking clearly in 2017. By the time 2019 ended, my credit was on life support. I also managed to save money. I learned the hard way to have money set aside. I found another agency called NACA to help me finance another home, but once I got into the program, I realized they were too deep in my business too soon in the relationship. I realized I was not ready even to consider getting a new home. Things were still too fresh for me to address financing another home.

Set Realistic Goals

My first goal was to live in our new apartment for 13 months. I thought I would be able to recoup some of the money I was owed after the sale of my home. However, I moved into the apartment; I realized it would be more difficult and expensive to tackle the mortgage and title companies.

My next goal was to continue to serve in the community. I would not have known Mr. Cooper ran their Hurricane Harvey Program for homeowners differently from Wells Fargo Bank's Harvey's Program if I had not volunteered to help Sweetie in Sunnyside. I believe it is possible to serve in the community and make money. I joined Pearland's Chamber of Commerce and the Brazoria County Hispanic Chamber of Commerce to increase my company's visibility in Pearland and generate revenue. People assumed I joined the chambers only for campaign purposes. I joined because Sam Walton said every businessperson should be a local chamber member because small businesses were the heart of a community. I also wanted to meet more women like myself through the chambers.

Next, I planned to generate more income before making more significant financial decisions. To increase my revenue, I needed to revampthe entire focus of my business and market them better. To update The Resource Center's mission, I completed two critical programs that helped me to rethink my business goals. First, I completed the Bank of America Institute for Women's Entrepreneurship at Cornell University. I learned new skills, more knowledge on how to grow my business, and I learned about new resources to finance my business. It was a great opportunity. I earned my certificationfrom an Ivy League program.

Then, I completed a 10-week online course called Selfmade Brit and Co. Brit Morin founded the program for female entrepreneurs to help them start or rethink their current business. The system was interactive and engaging. I loved meeting every week with all the ladies in the program. I still meet as an alumni member. It helped me realize I had not created or used a business plan when I started any business. I learned I failed to think out myvision. One of the best parts of the program for me was having access to it for life. We listened to some of the top female entrepreneurs like Bethenny Frankel, Gwyneth Paltrow, and tons of others. We were assigned a coach, and we learned how to make pitches and so many other things.

I missed my first office, and I knew I needed to secure another office space. I was determined to trust God to relocate my business. After attending both classes on entrepreneurship, I learned the location of my business mattered. I learned how to choose the best place for the services I offered. The Resource Center had a new mission and purpose after I became homeless. I had worked for seven years as the Principal of the Even Start Family Literacy Program. I loved working with adult students who wanted to learn English as a Second Language (ESL). We helped adult obtain their GED. We also taught toddlers and Pre-K students. We served mothers of all races to become their child's first and best teachers. Seventeen years later, I have beautiful friendships with my former secretary, Maria R., my former teachers, Mercedes W., and Maria V.

We have watched our children graduate and shared so many experiences. They were my first guests when I purchased my home, and they were there the day I moved from my house. I wanted to create an adult program that allowed adults to obtain education to help them become economically empowered. I wanted to have a team of great workers, and I needed an office to start the process. I moved in the new space May 2021.

I Learned to be Grateful

I learned to be grateful for the good and the bad things that happened. I learned to accept I had anxiety issues that needed to be addressed to focus and think clearly. I was grateful for deciding to put my mental health before my career. I was grateful when I finally resigned from the school district. I was thankful they gave me the push I needed to start a new job. I learned so much about myself during the process. I did not understand why it all happened, but I enjoyed things in life. I paid my mom for the time I stayed in her guest house. She did not ask me to, but I knew it was the thing to do. When I was able to get the AC fixed, I appreciated it more. I was also able to embrace the closeness of my family. I love our movie nights. We started new holiday traditions, and I hosted my first Thanksgiving and invited people outside of my immediate family. God restored communication and a friendship I thought was dead. I was also grateful for those relationships that ended. I had developed empathy and compassion for people who needed help to get back on their feet. I was not so quick to cast judgment on people. God showed me I play a significant role in shaping the next generation of Popes, so I needed to change.

When COVID-19 caused the schools to shut down, I did not panic about childcare. As a certified teacher, I helped my children with their online classes. I was thrilled I owned my own business. I worked to teach online courses. I was grateful for the COVID-19 funding provided for small business owners. I was able to utilize some of the funding options theSBA provided for small businesses.

Celebrate Small Wins

One of the most important things I learned while working to rebound from homelessness was that I needed to celebrate the small things.I am an overachiever, and I realized that I did not honor my small victories before I left the school district. Once I set a goal and achieve it, I move on to the next one without much fanfare. I never thought much about what it took to accomplish a purpose; I just became focused on finishing. Now, I celebrate the small and big events that happen in my life.

When I became homeless, I learned to enjoy cooking without a stove. I purchased a Ninja Food Grill. When I finally unpacked all my boxes, I celebrated. It took me a year to realize I was scared to unpack because I thought we might be evicted again. My family enjoyed a DQ Ice cream sandwich when we had a little extra money. When I worked with my children while they were at homeschooled, I learned to enjoy working with them. I look forward to seeing their grades. I participated in and celebrated their success. I celebrate when I stay awake the until the end of a movie during movie night. When I was a workaholic, I would not have taken the time to watch a movie with them.

I also started braiding my son's hair. He began to see I could do things he never imagined. I enjoyed trying new designs, and I looked forward to hearing the comments we received. I also celebrated when I made slight gains in my business. Eventually, I found joy again when I focused on the details and not the big picture, but I stayed present and in the moment. I celebrated when I took naps at 2:00 pm. I learned to listen to my body and treat it with more care. I celebrated when I realized my hair was naturally curly. I celebrated when I let my gray show; then, I celebrated when I dyed it again. I celebrated when I realized God had restored my hair's length. My children were so excited when they saw how long it had grown.

I hope my willingness to share my experiences with homelessness will help you avoid becoming homeless. I hope my story helps to erase the stereotypes about homeless people. I have five degrees, and I am drug-free, but I was homeless. I had a cell phone, a car, and clean clothes, but I had no address to call my own for 22 days. My fear of becoming homeless again for a year drove me to regroup my business. I also learned to ask for help. Being homeless leaves scars others cannot see, so carefully handle people you know are/were homeless.

I hope my story makes it easier for women to address their mental and physical health. There is no shame in asking for help, seeing a therapist, and extending forgiveness to others. Finally, I hope my story helps you ask for help whenever you feel you need it.

Bibliography

American Psychiatric Association, 2021, s.v. "anxiety disorder."

Associate Press. "Nationstar Mortgage to Refund $73M to Borrowers Under Order". December

    7, 2020, Accessed December 26, 2021. https://apnews.com/article/mortgages-charlotte-

    mortgage-insurance-87ac7284ad34f3569ce7943e83a055bd

Bekiempis, Victoria. "DMX's Official Cause of Death Revealed." *Vulture.com.* January 7, 2021.

    Accessed December 26, 2021. https://www.vulture.com/2021/07/dmx-cause-of-

    death.html

Boone, Keyaira. "The Glory of bell hooks will Live Forever-Revisit Some of Her Greatest Work

    Here." *Essence, 2021.* December 15, 2021, Accessed December 26, 2021.

    https://www.essence.com/culture/bell-hooks-books/

"Catch The Full DMX Verzuz Snoop Dogg Break Down Here," YouTube video, July 23, 2020,

    https://www.youtube.com/watch?v=XpYy_4_HwMw&t=4s

"DMX-Slippin (Official Music Video)," YouTube video, July 17, 2009.

    https://www.youtube.com/watch?v=9Ww-TQUeA3E

"DMX vs Snoop Dogg (Full Verzuz) on Instagram Live," YouTube video, July 23, 2020.

https://www.youtube.com/watch?v=9474VCdvNdw&t=1274s

Florida Condotel Mortgage. "Nationstar Mortgage Returning $86M to Homeowners".

December 8, 2020, Accessed December 26, 2021.

https://www.floridacondotelmortgage.com/nationstar-mortgage-returning-86m-to-

homeowners/

"Kanye West on "Donda" Drake, Marriage W/Kim Kardashian, His Legendary Career & More."

Drink Champs, November 4, 2021. Accessed December 26, 2021.

Leyes, Mark, and Maria Luisa Cesar. "DFPI Joins $88 Million Multi-State Settlement with

Nationstar Mortgage." CA.GOV. December 7, 2020, Accessed December 26, 2021,

https://dfpi.ca.gov/2020/12/07/dfpi-joins-88-million-multi-state-settlement-with-

nationstar-mortgage-llc/

Liber, Dave. "You Can Change a Troubled Company's Name, but Its Troubles Don't Go Away."

The Dallas Morning News, September 13, 2018, Accessed December 26, 2021,

https://www.dallasnews.com/news/watchdog/2018/09/13/you-can-change-a-troubled-

companys-name-but-its-troubles-dont-go-away/

Literary Devices. "Origin of The Lady Doth Protest Too Much." Literarydevices.net.

https://literarydevices.net/lady-doth-protest-too-

much/#:~:text=throughout%20the%20play.-

,Literary%20Devices,she%20remarries%20after%20king's%20death.

Oppenheim Law on Florida Law News, "Nationstar Rebrands as Mr. Cooper, but Can a Leopard

Change Its Spots?" South Florida Blog. September 25, 2017, Accessed December 26, 2021,

https://southfloridalawblog.com/nationstar-rebrands-mr-cooper-can-leopard-change-spots/

Oxford Language Google, 2021., s.v. "premise."

https://www.oxfordlearnersdictionaries.com/us/definition/american_english/premise

Perez, Lauren. "Mr. Cooper, Nationstar Faces Action Over Thousands of Unauthorized Mortgage

Payments." Top Class Actions. November 11, 2021, Accessed December 26, 2021.

https://topclassactions.com/lawsuit-settlements/money/loans/mr-cooper-nationstar-

faces-class-action-over-thousands-of-unauthorized-mortgage-payments/

Singletary, Michelle. "Nationstar Mortgage Agrees to a $91 Million Settlement for Mishandling

Foreclosures and Borrowers Payments." *The Washington Post,* December 8, 2020,

Accessed December 26, 2021.